Communication Skills II
COMM 10

Ms. Brandi Quesenberry | Course Guide Editor

Marlene M. Preston, PhD
Virginia Tech Department of Communication

Contents

	Page
Introduction	1
Course Materials	3
Syllabus	4
Grading Criteria	6
University Honor Code	7
Student Contributions	9
Resources	10
Communication with Faculty, Peers, and Professionals	11
Organizing for the Semester	13
Assignment chart -- Reflect and Comment	15
Unit I. Fundamentals of Formal Presentations	17
Unit II. Individual Research Project, Part 1: Informative Oral Report	41
Unit III. Individual Research Project, Part 2: Persuasive Written Report	59
Unit IV. Persuasive Group Presentations	67
Final – Collect, Reflect, Connect	89
Appendices	93
A. Progress Memo	
B. Informal feedback -- Stars and Wishes	
C. Course Development	

Academx

> Many thanks to the creative and dedicated faculty who have made this course so effective and who have offered suggestions to enhance this *Course Guide*.
>
> Our students and our department have benefited from your inspired work!

Communication Skills II Course Guide – COMM 1016, Spring 2019
Copyright © 2019 by Marlene M. Preston, PhD

Course Guide Editor: Ms. Brandi Quesenberry

All rights reserved. No part of this publication may be reproduced or transmitted in any form or by any means, electronic or mechanical, including photocopying, recording, or any information storage and retrieval system, without the written permission of the publisher.

Requests for permission to make copies of any part of the work should be mailed to:

Permissions Department
Academx Publishing Services, Inc.
P.O. Box 208
Sagamore Beach, MA 02562

Printed in the United States of America

ISBN-13: 978-1-68284-568-4
ISBN-10: 1-68284-568-0

Introduction to CommSkills II—Getting Started

Welcome back to CommSkills!

Congratulations on completion of the previous semester of CommSkills. CommSkills II will give you an opportunity to enhance your knowledge and skills even further and to reconnect with your classroom community. Since CommSkills II focuses more on research and public speaking, you will appreciate the support of that community as you approach these complex and very public tasks. You have many of the building blocks for a successful semester. Your interest and commitment will allow you to make the most of this year in CommSkills and to reap the benefits throughout your college coursework.

Please refresh your memory about the CommSkills course plan and goals. Consider the new goals specific to this semester so that you can personalize them when you write a progress memo. As you know, setting goals, monitoring progress, and reflecting on your accomplishment will help you get what you need from the course.

1015-1016 Course Description

This course sequence is designed for first-year students to satisfy requirements for Pathways Core1 (f). The goal of the courses is to develop practical discourse skills necessary for success in college and career such as interacting with teams, making in-class presentations, and communicating with peers, professors, and the public in person and in writing. Such skills include various types of communication required in the discourse community: interpersonal communication, group discussion, public speaking, listening, problem-solving, and audience-centered writing.

Through varied, practical experiences, students in Communication Skills will explore the transactional nature of communication through which people mutually and simultaneously cooperate to create shared meanings.

First, students will discover communication situations are more alike than different. All communication contexts are composed of the same basic characteristics, require similar basic skills, and involve the same principles and processes of communication, whether the context is public or private, formal or informal, collaborative or individual. Each context includes the same variables: organized messages, presentation skills (written, verbal, and nonverbal), and a transaction between sender and receiver.

Second, students will explore the unique characteristics that differentiate communication situations and will learn to adapt strategies and skills accordingly. The fundamental discourse skills and strategies--written, oral, visual, and nonverbal--developed in this course will be employed and refined throughout students' college and professional careers.

CommSkills and the University's Pathways to General Education

COMM 1015-1016 will fulfill requirements for Pathways Core1 (f) and any requirement for Public Speaking.

Pathways Core 1: Discourse Goals:
1. Discover and comprehend information from a variety of written, oral, and visual sources.
2. Analyze and evaluate the content and intent of information from diverse sources.
3. Develop effective content that is appropriate to a specific context, audience, and/or purpose.
4. Exchange ideas effectively with an audience.
5. Assess the product/presentation, including feedback from readers or listeners.

Goals for Both Semesters

Having successfully completed the two-course, six-hour sequence, students will be able to develop and present effective written and oral discourse in a range of communication contexts. They will develop and employ a repertoire of communication strategies that meet personal, professional, academic, and societal goals. Across two semesters, students will accomplish the following goals as they strive to become more effective and confident communicators:

- Analyze communication situations, including the relationships between and among presenter, audience, context
- Perform basic research, using print resources, on-line resources, and interviews
- Use steps of writing process to build oral and written presentations
- Develop and present messages effectively, adapting to the opportunities and constraints in a range of communication situations, including formal and informal, public and private, collaborative and individual
- Evaluate messages of self and others, employing critical listening and analysis tools
- Recognize ethical dimensions of discourse for presenter, audience, and context
- Explain the differences and connections between verbal (oral and written) and nonverbal communication channels
- Employ rhetorical sensitivity in intercultural, multicultural, and cross-cultural communication contexts
- Employ and choose appropriate technology and media for different goals and contexts

Goals Specific to Communication Skills II

The second semester of CommSkills will build on the topics studied during the COMM 1015 prerequisite. A successful student in this class will accomplish the following:

- Practice the basic types and principles of oral and written communication, including researched informative and persuasive presentations, proposal writing, and audience analysis
- Develop strategies for visual communication, including the use of presentation aids
- Identify and collect appropriate supporting materials for researched presentations while enhancing information literacy skills
- Develop documentation strategies, including integration of sources in to a text, using parenthetical citation, and building bibliographies
- Practice critical listening and thinking skills which will be reflected in writing and speaking
- Coordinate and contribute to a group research project, including group research, report development, and panel presentation
- Build skills for integrative learning

Competence in Writing, Critical Thinking, Information Literacy, Visual Expression, and Oral Communication

In addition to the specific goals of this course, Virginia Tech and the State Council for Higher Education in Virginia are committed to the development of student competence as part of this first-year experience. Over the past few years, students in CommSkills have helped the university provide assessment data to the State Council of Higher Education in Virginia. The course sequence has been included in the university assessment of writing competence, information literacy, oral communication competence, and critical thinking proficiency. (See partial list of standards below.) In each of these cases, students in produced work as a routine part of the course that was then included in a larger assessment initiative.

Overall, students have demonstrated high levels of proficiency by the end of COMM 1016. These skills will be documented in a course portfolio.

Virginia Tech has also developed a system for building students' skills across the four years of their undergraduate work. The development of Visual Expression, Writing, and Speaking (**ViEWS**) is part of the curriculum developed by each major. Participation in CommSkills is the first step along the ViEWS path.

Course Materials

Texts -- Required for all sections

Adler, R., Rodman, G., and du Pre, A. (2017). *Understanding human communication.* New York: Oxford University Press.

Howard, R. M. (2019). *Writing Matters* (3rd ed.), New York: McGraw-Hill.

Preston, M. (2019). *Course guide for Communication Skills* II. Virginia Beach, VA: Academx.

Various articles as assigned. (Articles will be available through library databases and Canvas and may be printed for classroom use.)

Course Guide. The *Course Guide* includes an overview of the course, some course policies, basic assignments and information about critiques. All instructors and students use these assignments in order to provide consistency across sections of the course. Instructors will provide policies unique to their sections and will adjust assignments as necessary. **While consistency across sections is a goal of this course sequence, individual instructors will customize assignments to meet the needs of students as the semester progresses.** Announcements of such changes will be made in class, sent on the class listserv, and/or posted on Canvas. Such announcements supersede any information found in this guide.

Supplies. Individual instructors will provide lists of supplies, such as a folder or index cards, which you must purchase for use during the semester.

Computer. Please check early in the semester to be sure that your computer and printer are fully functional. To participate fully in the course, you must be able to (1) send and receive e-mail, (2) access Canvas, and (3) explore electronic information sources. Instructors will assign articles to be obtained through various electronic sources.

Syllabus - Communication Skills II

The following sequence is tentative and may vary as the semester progresses. Dates for specific assignments will be provided in class. Formal writing and speaking assignments are shown in italics. Other reading assignments will be announced. Information from *Writing Matters* will be integrated throughout the semester. **Note: *Major writing and speaking assignments are shown below in bold and italics*.** All major assignments (*) must be completed so that a student may pass this class.

WM= *Writing Matters;* UHC= *Understanding Human Communication*

Topics (& approximate time frame)	Reading, *Writing and Speaking* Assignments	% of Grade
Introduction (Week 1)		
Introductions, course policies	*Course Guide*, Intro	
	Impromptu speaking; Integrative learning	
	Progress memo (Participation points)	
Unit I (Weeks 2-4 approx.)		
Fundamentals of Formal Presentations	Read sample essays as assigned	
Creating nonfiction narratives	WM, Review Parts 1 & 2 Informational Interview WM, 114; UHC, p. 306.	
Topic, audience – nonfiction narrative speeches; Informative Speaking	UHC, Ch. 11	
Organization and outlining	*Keyword Outline*	
Parenthetical citation – APA	***Documented essay*** * WM, in-text citation, Ch. 18; quotations, Ch. 53	10%
Delivery strategies	UHC, Ch. 12 (as assigned; questions on quiz with Unit II)	
Note cards, presentational aids	***Narrative speech**** *Peer evaluations*	5%
Quiz 1 – mult. choice & short answer	UHC & WM as assigned; sample essays	4%
Unit II (Weeks 5-8)		
Individual Research Project Part I Informative Speaking – Problem Building an argument	Read sample essays as assigned WM, Ch 11, Arguments UHC, Ch. 13	
Planning and implementing a research project; Evaluating electronic sources	WM, Ch. 13-16	
Considering needs of listeners	*Audience Analysis*	
Documentation – APA Style Bibliography & citing sources	WM, Ch. 24	
Developing documented informative speech with presentation aids	UHC, Ch. 13, pp. 380-386; WM, Ch. 9	
Informative speech -- problem	***Presentation plan, Informative researched speech, and bibliography****	15%
Quiz 2 – mult. choice & short answer	UHC & WM as assigned; essays & speeches	4%

Unit III (Weeks 8-11)

Individual Research Project Part II Persuasive Writing -- Solution	Read sample essays as assigned	
Needs of listeners vs. readers	Audience analysis (from Unit II)	
Characteristics of persuasion	UHC Ch. 14 (consider strategies for speeches that can also work in writing)	
Developing documented paper Documentation – APA style Use of visuals in text	WM, Chapter 17 & 18 WM, Ch. 23 & 26 Ch. 7c visuals	
Persuasive report -- solutions	*Outline; Persuasive researched report,* Peer evaluations*	20%
Quiz 3 – mult. choice & short answer	UHC & WM as assigned; sample essays & speeches	4%

Unit IV (Weeks 11-15)

Group Persuasive Presentations	Read sample essays as assigned	
Review of group discussion skills	UHC, Ch. 9	
Characteristics of persuasive presentations	Review UHC, Ch. 10	
Planning a group research project	*Proposal with audience analysis,* WM chp. 5	
	Group Presentation with Bibliography,*	15%
	Presentation plan, Peer and self evaluations	
Quiz 4 -- mult. choice & short answer	UHC & WM as assigned; sample essays	4%

"Exam" and Participation

Final *Integrative Learning* *Check Timetable for exam date and time!*	*Informal speech; Reflection essay;* *Portfolio: Collect, Reflect, Connect – with Resume*—WM, chapter 8b	10%
Participation	Class participation	8%
	Required research participation	1%

The following activities will be defined by instructors and may include various types of activities, any of which will yield participation points.

Writing activities include any of the following: Electronic communication; informal writing of exit slips, memos, informal responses, peer evaluations; reflection; journal writing; written summaries of in-class group work, or Weekly Writing Works (WWW).

Speaking activities include any of the following: impromptu speeches; building interpersonal relationships with faculty and peers; and in-class group work

Research activities are integral parts of this course. **Secondary research** will involve your analysis and selection of supporting materials from library databases and other electronic sources to build your informative and persuasive projects. **Primary research** will include your use of surveys and/or interviews as tools for gathering information.

<u>Another form of primary research will include your involvement in a departmentally approved project for which you will receive credit as part of your participation grade.</u> While you help faculty, graduate students, and advanced undergraduate students complete research projects, you will also contribute to the development of knowledge in the discipline of communication. *In terms of your personal growth, you will learn about ethical standards and research methods used at the college level.* This experience should help as you consider your own research.

Grading Criteria for Formal Assignments

Consider the following criteria as you review your graded work. Of course, graded work will be accompanied by notes from your instructor, indicating the strengths of your oral or written presentation and suggestions for further development of your writing skills. Seek clarification of these comments if they are not clear to you or if you have questions about the grading practices.

Average Presentation "C"	Good Presentation "B"	Superior Presentation "A"
1. **Format:** conforms to the assignment's length and format	1. **Format:** conforms to the assignment's length and format	1. **Format:** conforms to the assignment's length and format
2. **Organization:** exhibits appropriate organization	2. **Organization:** exhibits appropriate organization	2. **Organization:** exhibits appropriate organization
3. **Accuracy:** includes appropriate language and correct grammar	3. **Accuracy:** includes appropriate language and correct grammar	3. **Accuracy:** includes appropriate language and correct grammar
4. **Support:** demonstrates competent use of supporting data	4. **Support:** demonstrates competent use of supporting data	4. **Support:** demonstrates competent use of supporting data
5. **Outline:** accompanies correctly formatted outline	5. **Outline:** accompanies correctly formatted outline	5. **Outline:** accompanies correctly formatted outline
	6. **Style:** arouses audience interest and understanding through appropriate style and expression	6. **Style:** arouses audience interest and understanding through appropriate style and expression
	7. **Visuals:** designs and incorporates effective visuals	7. **Visuals:** designs and incorporates effective visuals
	8. **Logic:** establishes supported and documented logic and reasoning	8. **Logic:** establishes supported and documented logic and reasoning
	9. **Credibility:** enhances the presenter's credibility as a competent and dynamic writer or speaker	9. **Credibility:** enhances the presenter's credibility as a competent and dynamic writer or speaker
		10. **Creativity:** constitutes a genuinely individual, creative contribution in topic and development appropriate for a specific audience
		11. **Rhetoric:** achieves a skillful mastery of rhetorical concepts
		12. **Language:** demonstrates vivid and precise use of language

Grading Scale
Please ask your instructor to explain the grading scale, which is generally the following:

A-	90-92	A	93-97	A+	98-100
B-	80-82	B	83-87	B+	88-89
C-	70-72	C	73-77	C+	78-79
D-	60-62	D	63-67	D+	68-69
F	0-59				

Observance of the Honor Code

Honesty in your academic work makes you a trustworthy member of the class and also builds ethical habits for your professional career. The honor code will be strictly enforced in this course. All assignments submitted shall be considered graded work. All aspects of your coursework are covered by the honor system. The faculty and students of Virginia Tech will not tolerate any form of academic dishonesty. Conduct yourself in an ethical manner, and you will have no concerns about violating the Honor Code.

Thoroughly review the following sections about the University Honor System and plagiarism to familiarize yourself with the possible problems.

University Honor System

Students enrolled in this course are responsible for abiding by the Honor Code. Any student who has doubts about how the Honor Code applies to any assignment is responsible for obtaining specific guidance from the course instructor before submitting the assignment for evaluation. Ignorance of the rules does not exclude any member of the University community from the requirements and expectations of the Honor Code.

> **The Undergraduate Honor Code Pledge** that each member of the University Community agrees to abide by states:
> "As a Hokie, I will conduct myself with honor and integrity at all times. I will not lie, cheat, or steal, nor will I accept the actions of those who do."

For additional information about the Honor Code, please visit: http://honorsystem.vt.edu/

Plagiarism

Plagiarism is just one type of academic misconduct, and it may take many forms, each of which is unacceptable. According to the Virginia Tech Honor System, "Plagiarism includes the copying of the language, structure, programming, computer code, ideas, and/or thoughts of another and passing off the same as one's own original work, or attempts thereof."

Any written or oral work you present as your own for this class should be completely your own--content, organization, language choices, visuals--unless you cite the sources from which you have borrowed ideas. This includes work completed in conjunction with peer reviews or tutors; reviewers might offer advice, but students must write their own work for submission.

Resources - Plagiarism and Consequences
- "Ethics and Communication" – stressed throughout your texts
- *Writing Matters* – Ch. 16
- Virginia Tech Library: http://www.lib.vt.edu/help/plagiarism.html

Potential Plagiarism Problems

The following examples--adapted from a list by Dr. Rachel Holloway, Vice Provost, Virginia Tech--illustrate areas in which students might make ethical errors with their oral or written presentations. Although this is not an exhaustive list, it does identify the most frequent of such dishonest behaviors.

Representation of someone else's words or ideas without acknowledgment of the original source --
This includes exact quotation, paraphrase of ideas, duplication of organizational design, recounting of narratives, or other content, without appropriate attribution. A student may avoid plagiarism by citing the source of the materials in the speech performance. Simply including the sources on a bibliography without clear citation in the speech or paper misrepresents the origin of the ideas/materials to the immediate audience and would constitute plagiarism. Carefully document your sources; avoid even flirting with plagiarism.

Representation of visual or graphic materials as one's own work when they are either duplicated from some other source or created with the help of another individual --
The Honor System bans "work for hire" or "purchased work." This does not mean that you are forbidden to use technology to prepare visual aids. The key, again, is to give appropriate credit to the original source of the material.

Use of "file" speeches or papers --
Your presentations are to be the product of your original research, thought, and composition. Simply rephrasing or reordering the ideas, organization, supporting materials, or any other element of a presentation from someone else's preparation and materials does not meet the requirements of original work and is an honor code violation. Extemporaneous delivery of a stolen or borrowed speech does not exempt a student from plagiarism charges.

Use of a misleading bibliography to "document" your speech --
A bibliography must include only the materials used in the development of the presentation. Inclusion of materials that were not used for analysis or incorporated into a presentation constitutes a violation.

Peer Review and Group Work
Often during this semester, you will be participating in pairs or groups to work on some aspect of an assignment. Be sure you have a clear understanding of which parts of the project are to be completed by individuals and which parts are to be completed by the entire group. Check with your instructor for clarification if necessary. You should save all facets of your work so that you can verify your own contributions to a presentation.

When in Doubt . . .
If at any time you have a question about your preparation and the honor code, it is your responsibility to review the resources and/or check in class. Ignorance is not a defense for plagiarism.

Student Contributions

1. Prepare! The university standard requires approximately two hours of outside work for every hour spent in class. Read the material assigned and carefully review class notes. Preparation time will also be spent constructing speeches and researching.

Always come to class prepared to discuss the assigned reading shown on the syllabus.

2. Participate! Your **courtesy** and attention to other students and to your instructor are crucial components of this class. Your increasing skill in communication should be reflected in your tolerance of diverse opinions and your ability to express your own opinions. Review the VT Principles of Community at http://www.vt.edu/diversity/principles-of-community.html

Your **presence** in class is crucial because of the experiential nature of this class. You need the information presented in lectures, you need the experience of observing other speakers, and you need to make presentations.

Your **preparation** for class will be revealed in class discussions and activities. Your partnership with peers will be revealed in your active listening to their speeches. (Just as you will depend on your classmates for their attention and feedback, so they will depend on you.) Your understanding of effective communication will be revealed in your oral and written critiques of others' speeches. All of these activities will have an impact on your participation grade.

Policies related to attendance and cancellation of classes will be discussed at the first class meeting and posted online.

3. Present! Present oral and written assignments that you have thoroughly prepared. Your careful crafting of appropriate material and your enthusiastic delivery will ensure an interested audience and a good grade.

Policies related to missed presentations will be discussed at the first class meeting and posted online.

4. Problem-solve! When you're feeling confused or overwhelmed, you must make use of the resources available to assist you with the problem. The semester moves quickly, so you must act as soon as you identify a problem. To identify resources, begin at the Virginia Tech homepage (www.vt.edu). Consider any of the following:
- Self -- texts, notes, Course Guide, organization and time management
- Instructor -- e-mail, discussion opportunities in and out of class, office hours
- Classmates -- making connections and using the listserv
- Library - resources related to all aspects of communication and research
- Presentation resources -- See next page.
- Computer labs, support - Use "4help" for assistance with your e-mail or technology.
- Office of Academic Enrichment - for tutoring
- Counseling Services - for assistance with personal problems
- Student Affairs Office - for support with campus life problems and disabilities

Note: If you have a documented learning disability, please alert your instructor as soon as possible. Necessary accommodations will be provided to foster your success.

Resources
Take the initiative to help yourself by using resources designed to support your learning. Ask your instructor to send you an electronic list of the following websites or to post the list online.

Writing
- **Online resources connected to *Writing Matters*** -- supplemental information, practice exercises, examples.
- **The Writing Center** -- The Writing Center is a free writing tutorial and consultation service for students, faculty, and staff.
- **Online Writing Lab (OWL)** -- Includes Grammar Hotline and Electronic Tutoring
- **Write101.com** -- Visit this site to find many tips to improve your writing. Check the archives for short references on punctuation, confused words, and other troubling writing issues. You can even subscribe to a weekly electronic newsletter for a tip of the week (your own WWW)!

Note about peer reviews: Please take advantage of any resources, but be sure to own your work! Don't let a reviewer re-write your work or even correct it without your understanding of any problems. Your goal in getting help should be to learn how to improve your writing. If others rewrite your paper and you turn it in, you're participating in an unethical process and submitting others' work as your own. See the section in this Course Guide about plagiarism.

Speaking
- **CommLab** -- A resource for student speakers in Newman Library where peer coaches assist students with development and rehearsal of speeches
    Visit **www.commlab.vt.edu or contact commlab@vt.edu**

Study Skills -- See the Counseling Center website for information about test-taking, time management, memory, test anxiety, approaches to textbooks, relaxation, etc.

Technology – Lynda.com -- http://www.olcs.lt.vt.edu/lynda/index.html -- This is a free resource for various programs that you may want to learn, including Word and PowerPoint.

Research, documentation, ethics
Familiarizing yourself with the library and its services will be one of the most important gifts you ever give to yourself! Last semester, you visited the library to get a sense of the library's geography and to check out a book. This semester, you will build on that knowledge as you develop strategies to search the library's database. Understanding the library will help you as your work your way through Virginia Tech; understanding sophisticated electronic search strategies will help you forever! *Note: If you were unable to schedule a library tour last semester, your instructor will require you to complete a tour so that you move forward with the rest of this library work.*
- Bookmark the Newman Library homepage: **http://www.lib.vt.edu/**
- Click on the last link under "Research Skills": "Services for Students" -- You'll see a wealth of information designed for students to help them complete projects and access the library easily.
- See "Six Steps to Library Research" -- You'll find a good overview of the research process with many helpful hints about college-level research.
- See the informative and interactive information on "Evaluating Web Resources" -- This page will provide useful information to help you evaluate and justify the use of any web resource.
- Try the Information Skills modules or the Research Paper scheduler.
- Check "Citation and Style Manuals" for information about documenting sources

Communication with Faculty and Peers -- *Practice Professionalism!*

As you enhance your communication skills, you will feel more and more comfortable contacting faculty and peers with questions or concerns about the class or campus. Please review the instruction about e-mail and netiquette that you received last semester.

Contacting Faculty

Faculty at Virginia Tech want to help you. Consider your communication options, and try to determine a professor's preference. Some are quick to respond to e-mail while others would prefer to talk to you in person or on the phone.

Phone calls and messages
- Use the phone numbers provided by the professor in class or on the course syllabus.
- Identify yourself! Don't assume that a professor knows which class you are in or why you're calling.
- Keep messages short, and leave your phone number.

Personal/business/academic e-mail to a professional
- Show respect for your reader's time by sending only necessary e-mail.
- Use the same formal tone and structure you would use in a memo.
- Use a precise word or phrase for the subject line.
- Use a title for an attachment that reflects your name and/or the assignment title. Be sure that your name is also on the document itself.

Office visits
- Check office hours or make an appointment.
- Clarify your reason for the visit if you need to discuss something specific. Plan ahead to be sure you'll cover any questions you need to ask.
- Be mindful of appropriate body language and tone.

Contacting Class Members - class listserv

Work to develop relationships with other students so that you can support each other outside class.
- Use the class listserv only for any message that relates to class content or community.
- Your message will be sent to everyone in the class, so avoid personal messages that apply only to your group members or one other individual.
- Do not forward chain mail or any announcements with which you have no personal connections.
- Review the guidelines concerning netiquette (discussed in COMM 1015). Your classmates trust you!
- When replying to a listserv message, remember that your response will go to the whole class. Address your response to an individual if only one person needs to get your message.

Email Standards for Professionals

Standards for electronic communication are still evolving, but standards DO exist. Despite the popularity of IM and Twitter, email is still the standard in professional (academic or workplace) settings. As with any communication, the level of formality is dictated by your MAP. You've been using a class listserv or a chat function on Canvas as you have communicated with your instructor and your classmates. While that may seem to be rather informal communication, it still is slightly more formal than your text or social media messages to your friends and family.

The following notes describe strategies for professional email. Keep in mind that email to a professional is similar to a business memo or letter. Your instructor will review the details with you so that you can create effective messages to faculty and other professionals.

Settings
   Sender's name and choice of email account
   - Real name (upper and lower case), not PID -- Adjust your settings to reflect your whole name.
   - Sender's email address should enhance credibility – Use your vt.edu account when your message involves your work as a Virginia Tech student.

   Signature line to enhance credibility
   - 4-8 short lines
   - Provide contact info

Subject line (borrowed from memo form)
   - Concise, precise; No false urgency

Body
   Technicalities
   - Avoid underlining, bold, all caps, anything cutesy
   - Use correct grammar, punctuation, spelling
   - Skip a line between paragraphs

   Salutation (borrowed from letter form)
   - Use "Dear" and/or the recipient's title for more formal email
   - Specific reader's name - reflecting level of formality
   - Use correct titles for faculty - Mr., Dr., Mrs. - along with a last name, not a first name

   Message
   - Concise, concise, concise
   - Sign off with your whole name, not a nickname
   - Refer to any attachments in a short message; entitle attachment for reader's convenience

Responding to email
   - Respond carefully to sensitive messages; take time to prepare your response
   - Respond quickly to routine messages
   - Retain at least part of the previous message so that reader can review sequence
   - Current author places message at the top so that reader sees current message first
   - Take a cue from your correspondent's level of formality

Organizing for the Semester

To prepare yourself for the semester, be sure that you have all course materials and set the stage for your work by completing the following tasks.

I. Prepare to Research and Print!
Articles: Throughout this semester, you will be asked to find articles for in-class discussion or personal reference. These essays will serve as examples for your own writing. While the CommSkills faculty could have selected an anthology of essays to provide essay examples (and required that you purchase it), they decided not to because of the following considerations:
- A "reader" (published collection) would have been expensive and limited in terms of types of essays and currency of essays.
- The use of articles allows us to explore current and relevant essays from a variety of sources.
- Your search for articles helps you to build proficiency with the library databases.

Yes, you may be asked to print some of these articles, but in the end, you will have saved some money on an extra textbook AND enhanced your research skills!

II. Create a personal editing checklist
Create a list of reminders for your use when you are writing a paper. Use the following as a guide, see the lists in *Writing Matters* or create your own. To identify problem areas, review your portfolio from last semester. You've received a wealth of feedback that should help you create a New Year's Writing Resolution! Your instructor may ask you to put this list in your folder too.

Prewriting
- Brainstorming for topic or focus
- Sufficient prewriting to develop focus and rich details

Organization and Drafting
- Appropriate format
- Attention to MAP
- Intro with thesis
- Topic sentences for body paragraphs
- Development with specific and vivid details
- Transitions--beginning of body paragraphs &within paragraphs

Technical and stylistic considerations
- WWW problems -- Confused words
- Comma splices
- Agreement Sentence variety
- Modifiers
- Commas

III. Consider your progress and plan to integrate your learning (see next page)

IV. Attach "Reflect and Comment" page to your folder (p. 15)

Progress Memo

Real learning requires mindfulness. In order to get the most from your classes, you need to consider the big picture – not just isolated assignments or quizzes.

For this reason, you use a folder in CommSkills to collect your work so that you and your instructor can both easily review your writing/speaking strengths and weaknesses.

In COMM 1015, you completed a Goals Memo and then worked across the semester to meet those goals. You also reflected on your accomplishments in your final essay.

In COMM 1016, you'll complete a progress report so that you can get some perspective on the goals you've completed, the ones still in progress, and the ones you still need to address. Your instructor may choose to assign this memo early in the semester, at midterm, or as part of your self-evaluation in the research units. At the end of the semester, you'll reflect on your growth across the year. The completed Progress Memo will be one of the assignments you'll consider as you write that final essay.

The directions for the Progress Memo can be found in Appendix A.

Integrative Learning

According to the American Association of Colleges and Universities, "Integrative learning is an understanding and a disposition that a student builds across the curriculum and co-curriculum, from making simple connections among ideas and experiences to synthesizing and transferring learning to new, complex situations within and beyond the campus" (www.aac&u.org).

Do you want to be valuable in your academic, social, civic, and professional settings? If so, now is the time to start looking for the connections between the areas of your life. What you're learning in one class will be useful in another class, in your relationships, in the voting booth, or at your internship. The experiences you're having may be important in isolation, but if you work toward integrating the knowledge you're accumulating, you'll be stronger in many ways.

If you're "Just Scoring Points" (as noted in the article you may have read in the fall), you're really not getting your money's worth from your college education. Yes, you'll end up with a diploma, but the information your accumulated will be disjointed, hard to access, and won't be so handy when you really need it. You may have gotten an "A" on a test, but the learning may not have been categorized, associated with other information, or stored in long-term memory.

Try to assess your strengths now, and plan to develop an even greater capacity for recognizing and using the connections between your courses, your relationships, and your activities. Doing so, will help you to maximize the value you get from your college education so that you graduate with a rich understanding of the world, its interconnectedness, and your place in it.

At the end of this semester, you'll be reflecting on your skill with integrative learning.

Unit I -- *Fundamentals of Formal Presentations*
Non-fiction Writing and Speaking

Goals
As you complete this unit you will
- develop critical analysis skills
- recognize and apply appropriate organizational patterns for narratives
- enhance delivery skills
- practice creation and use of presentational aids
- practice essay format
- enhance skill with correct and effective writing
- develop interviewing skills
- practice integration of quotes into text and APA documentation style

Formal Assignments
_____**Part I -- Written Presentation – Non-fiction narrative essay**
- Evidence of writing process
- Peer review
- Essay with direct quotes
    (Parenthetical citation and bibliography in APA style only required if sources include more than one interview.)

Part II -- Oral Presentation – Non-fiction narrative speech
_____**A. Presentation plan**
- Preliminary paperwork -- brainstorming, rough draft of outline
- Final draft -- keyword outline form including MAP

_____**B. Narrative Speech presentation**
- Speech content, organization
- Speech delivery and visual aid

Other requirements
Reading assignments – See Syllabus and Canvas for text references and assigned essays.

Unit I Quiz grade – *Writing Matters, Understanding Human Communication*, essays

Peer Critiques – You earn participation points for each assigned peer critique.

Unit I, Part 1 -- Written Presentation – Nonfiction Narrative Essay

This semester we'll be reading nonfiction essays and writing some of our own. For this assignment, you will conduct an interview of someone who has a true story to share. Then you will tell that story in an essay. This essay will be biographical in nature (as you tell another person's story); our subsequent assignment – the narrative speech – may be autobiographical (a personal story of your own) or biographical.

Your instructor will provide further guidelines about the essay, including possible approaches, audiences, and purposes for such an essay.

Your instructor will also offer direction to help you choose a good interview subject – maybe a hero, a family member with an intriguing story, a favorite coach, a remarkable friend you've met at VT. Maybe you'll take this opportunity to track down the real story behind a family legend – one that you hear about every year when your families get together. Maybe you'll get your grandfather to tell you the details about something that happened to him as a young man.

Because you'll be writing an essay, not a book, you'll need to focus on one experience, hobby, or adventure this person has had. You'll interview this person, and then you'll use your notes to build an essay. You might collect newspaper articles that were written at the time or photos that could also be used to support your essay. The essay might also connect to one of our texts.

In class, we'll be discussing interview techniques, the use of direct quotations in your writing, the use of dialogue, and the appropriate way to cite an interview in a bibliography. Your mastery of these skills will be important as we move through the semester. Your instructor will also direct you to some nonfiction essays that include narration and biography so that you can see how other writers have handled this challenge.

The essay should include the following:
- A story about someone you know well and can interview
- Your personal perspective about the story, supported by information from your own research – your interview and any other documentation you might find
- Hallmarks of the narrative including organization, conflict, and meaning (See discussion in *Course Guide*.)
- At least one direct quotation and one indirect quotation -- both with parenthetical citations

Process:
   Planning the interview
- Brainstorm ideas for subjects. Make a list of people in your life who could be likely subjects for an interview. Consider stories you've heard about people's accomplishments, hardships, or adventures.
- Choose a subject who is willing to chat with you and accessible. The better you know this person, the easier it will be for you to decide on a focus for your interview. Choose a time in that person's life that is unusual or intriguing for some reason.

From Outline to Draft for College Essays -- CommSkills, History, Biology, etc.

Essay Components	Section of outline-->	becomes part of draft
Title -- Engage the readers (not name of assignment)		Surprise; Connection between writer and readers; Question; Intriguing background
Intro parag -- Engage the readers	MAP	To engage your readers, • Open with attention-getter • Connect with your readers • Include intriguing detail • Spotlight (not floodlight) the main focus (See note below about thesis)
Body of essay--each parag		Open with a transition
	Roman numeral (I, II, III)	Topic sentence (1st or 2nd sentence of parag)
	Letter (A, B, C)	2-3 sentences (minimum) for each supporting detail; use vivid, specific detail with sensory appeal
		Use a transition before each new point (From A to B; From B to C)
		No conclusion sentence necessary for most body parag; might be effective in longer or more scientific paper
Conclusion		Emphasize the thesis; don't repeat it if you've already stated it in the intro parag. • No new supporting details • Don't list main points in short essays • End with memorable thought

Placement of Thesis

While most essays include the thesis at the end of the intro paragraph, narrative essays might open with some action and context-setting. In that case, a thesis might be at the end of the essay.

In either case, your thesis should. . .
- Suggest focus of whole essay; entire essay will prove this statement
- Include reference to content and focus or attitude
- NOT include a list of main points

Managing the Main Points -- Audience of Listeners or Readers?

Speeches -- Speakers depend on the "Ministerial Three," the organizational pattern that a minister uses in a sermon: He tells you what he's going to tell you; he tells you; then he tells you what he told you. Listeners benefit from the use of this pattern because it helps them to organize and remember the information as they hear it. They almost fill in the blanks while listening.

Essays -- Writers can be more subtle than speakers because readers control the flow of information. They can stop reading at any point, or they can go back and re-read an idea that intrigued them or puzzled them. Writers can avoid the "baseball bat" approach, hitting the readers over the head with the repetition of the main points three times -- intro, body and conclusion. An intelligent reader can grasp the main points without this overt repetition.

You may have learned this strategy in high school because your teachers were helping you to organize your papers. More sophisticated writers usually suggest the focus of the essay, address the main ideas, and then conclude by emphasizing the main focus of the whole essay.

Think carefully about audience needs.
Readers and listeners receive information in different ways.

Feedback -- Providing Feedback to Others

Value of Critiques
Peer critiques are useful to the writer or speaker and also to the reviewer. Reviewers not only earn participation points, but they also gain practice with analysis, problem-solving, and tactful expression of ideas.

Tone of Critiques
Students often say that they are not qualified to write critiques, they don't want to criticize their friends, and they don't want to make notes about other students' drafts or speeches. You'll learn to write good critiques! You'll get better and better at finding the words to effectively, honestly, AND tactfully characterize the strengths and weaknesses in a presentation. Make comments that will help the presenter maintain the effective aspects of speaking and improve the weak aspects. Avoid being vicious or syrupy sweet. Either extreme is useless to the speaker or writer. Be constructive!

Completing Critiques of Written Work
- Use the forms supplied in the *Course Guide* or in class for any peer critiques of written work.
- Spend your allotted time focusing on all components of the written work: organization, content, style, grammar, and mechanics. Avoid spending most of your time on spelling errors that will be cleaned up in subsequent drafts.
- Offer your advice on an evaluation sheet, rather than on the draft. Minimally mark the draft itself. **Don't correct the work or rewrite it.** You are not an editor.
- Focus on stars and wishes; then discuss your comments with the writer.

Feedback -- Receiving and Processing Feedback from Others

Peer Feedback
Peer feedback during developmental stages of your work is also very important. When we look at our own work, we often see what we meant to write rather than what we really did write. Peer reviewers can spot errors that authors often overlook. They also can ask questions and point out gaps in logic or sequence. If several peers review your work, you will gain insight from the audience perspective and many suggestions for improvement.

Reading Critiques of Written Work
If the feedback you receive is on a rough draft, carefully weigh any resulting changes you make. Your peer reviewer has made suggestions, not mandates. You are ultimately responsible for the presentation of your final draft.

Please be sure that your reviewers are not rewriting your work! When you submit your final draft, the language and ideas should be yours!

Unit I, Part 2 -- Nonfiction Narrative Speech

Requirement
    Narrative speech:
- Based on a true event in someone's life (autobiographical or biographical)
- Limited in scope so that you can include specific and vivid detail
- Meaningful to target audience
- Clearly exhibiting biographical or autobiographical significance
- Delivered in extemporaneous style

    Time: 3-5 minutes

Speech preparation: In general, you will be asked to complete the following steps:
- Choose an appropriate topic
- Determine audience needs
- Generate supporting detail
- Organize
- Formulate introduction, transitions, and conclusion
- Design and create a presentation aid according to guidelines discussed in class
- Rehearse
- Present, using a 4X6 note card
- Evaluate

Related writing
- Presentation plan or outline
- Peer critiques

Related reading -- See Syllabus and Canvas

Narrative Speech
    Many speakers use stories to illustrate main ideas. Those stories may be entertaining, informational, or inspirational. Build a speech around a true event that was meaningful in your life. Explain why the incident is significant to you (autobiographical) or to your interviewee (biographical). If you use the same topic for your essay and your speech, be sure to choose a different audience for the speech. Demonstrate your understanding of audience-based decision-making – details, language choice, explanation of context, etc.
    This speech establishes your credibility for upcoming speeches and allows you to test your speaking ability. Since no further research is required for this speech, you'll be able to focus on organization and delivery. You might even have fun with this presentation!
    As an audience member for peer speakers, you'll also have the opportunity to build (1) your skills as an evaluator and (2) a better understanding of your classmates.

Narrative or Informative? Both! Essentially the narrative genre dictates your organization. You're telling a story. Because this story is nonfiction, you're using narrative to inform your audience about an event. The *Understanding Human Communication* text provides lots of good tips for informative speaking.

Steps in Preparing Your Narrative Speech
Visit CommLab at some point in the process!

Develop a topic and supporting details

    Find a topic – For an autobiographical topic, use your personal brainstorming or suggestions of friends and family. Generate a list of possibilities from which you might choose. For a biographical topic, review your interview notes.

    Choose a meaningful story with some biographical or autobiographical significance. Usually such a story had some impact and still brings back feelings of joy, surprise, anger, sadness, etc. Narrow your focus to one specific event, one part of a trip, or one afternoon at the beach.

    Note: You may want to build this speech from the documented essay you wrote. If so, you should significantly alter your approach – new audience, decisions make for listeners rather than readers – so that you avoid reading an essay written for readers instead of a speech prepared for listeners.

    Freewrite -- Sketch out the story. Jot down details as you try to recreate the incident. Who was there? What did those people say? What were the sights, sounds, smells? How did the main character (you or your interviewee) feel? Surprises? Anger? Laughter? Reaction? Long-term effect?

    Narrow the focus -- You'll be able to use lots more specific detail if you're careful to narrow the focus. If your topic is too broad, you'll be racing to cover the events with no time to describe the scene or the people. Try focusing on something that happened in one day or on one weekend. Check your MAP decisions as another way of narrowing the focus. <u>For this narrative speech assignment, your audience will be your classmates.</u> Select a focus that they can relate to.

    Sharpen the details -- Review the characteristics of narratives as described earlier in this *Course Guide*. Will your story fit the general pattern of a narrative? Clarify your story by discussing it with a friend or listing the basic components of the incident. Focus on a clear description of the basic conflict. Omit unnecessary or confusing details. Make characters and locations seem real. Use names and concrete descriptive terms. Add realistic dialogue. Consider one aspect of the story that could be enhanced through the use of a visual.

    Clarify (auto)biographical significance -- Story-tellers try to make a point with the story. They try to share a perception about life based on this experience. As you build a narrative, consider why you want to tell this story, and why does your listener want to hear it? How was it important to the main character (you or your interviewee)? What difference did it make in someone's life? How does it exemplify some larger truth about life? While you need to make this clear in your speech, avoid "so the moral of my story is. . . " Often speakers allude to this significance in the intro and then make it clear in the conclusion.

Countdown to Narrative Speeches

Note card

Prepare your note card with key words and phrases. Crowded note cards are no help when you're looking for a quick reminder of a main point. You may want to number your cards and maybe even color-code them. Note cards may be collected after your speech.

Presentation aid -- an object

Refine your presentation aid. Make it big, and keep it simple. For this speech, choose an object, a poster, or an enlarged photograph. We'll practice in later speeches with PowerPoint.

Practice holding this object at shoulder height so that all members of the audience will be able to see it. Reveal it at a particular point in the speech, and then remove it from view so that it does not distract the audience. Don't plan to pass this object around the room during your speech. If you do need to distribute something to the class, such as a handout or memento of your speech, provide access at the end of the speech.

Rehearsal

Practice and time your speech at least twice with an audience. Ask for feedback. Work toward a conversational (not read or memorized) style. You must observe the time limits given for each speech. You will be allowed a thirty-second grace period. Aside from that, your grade will reflect any failure to abide by the limits. If you practice and become comfortable with your speech, you'll have a better chance of achieving the length required.

As you practice, work on your delivery style. Use your note card and your object. The extemporaneous delivery allows you to develop eye contact, facial and vocal expression, and gestures, all of which keep your audience interested. For these reasons, you will not use a lectern to deliver your speech. You want to establish a rapport with your audience, not hide behind barriers.

> Contact CommLab for an appointment if you want some tips from the coaches or you want to practice in front of people. This can help you feel more comfortable by the time you present your speech in class. For an appointment: www.commlab.vt.edu

On the Day of the Speech
- Allow yourself time for breakfast and one run-through of the speech.
- Consider your appearance. This is an informal speech, so your appearance should be neat and casual. NO HATS!
- Bring required components to class. Your instructor will have specified such items as the following:
    - Final draft of your presentation plan, stapled or clipped to any drafts, freewriting, brainstorming (final draft on top)
    - Instructor critique form
    - Note card (4x6) -- after the speech
- As you wait in class for your turn to present, practice square breathing or any relaxation exercise that helps you.

Speech Competencies and Critiques

Following is a list of general competencies that will be considered for each oral presentation. These same components will be considered for each speech this semester with the addition of specifics relevant to narrative, informative and persuasive speeches. This list is adapted with permission from the "Competent Speaker" Speech Evaluation Form by Sherwyn Morreale, Michael Moore, K. Phillip Taylor, Donna Surges-Tatum, and Ruth Hulbert-Johnson (1993). "The Competent Speaker" was developed by the National Communication Association Committee for Assessment and Testing and representatives of 12 academic institutions.

Competencies:

1. Topic and Connection with Audience
Selection and narrowing of a topic appropriate for audience and occasion.

2. Thesis/Specific Purpose
Clarification of the thesis and/or specific purpose in a manner appropriate for the audience and occasion.

3. Support
    a. Supporting material -- use of examples, details, research, and/or argument, appropriate for the audience and occasion.
    b. Presentational aids -- design of visual and/or audio support to enhance the speech, including the use of PowerPoint, objects, handouts, etc.

4. Organization
Use of an organizational pattern appropriate to topic, audience, occasion & purpose.
- Introduction with attention-getter, connection with audience, preview or focus statements
- Organization enhanced with transitions
- Conclusion with impact

5. Language
Use of language appropriate to the audience, occasion & purpose

6. Vocal Variety
Use of vocal variety in rate, pitch & intensity to heighten and maintain interest

7. Vocal Accuracy (Intelligibility)
Use of accurate pronunciation, grammar, & articulation

8. Physical Behaviors -- Use of movement & gestures that support the message, including eye contact; facial expression; sincerity, warmth, enthusiasm, natural gesture, posture, movement; appropriate use of notes; and appropriate appearance

Completing Critiques of Speeches

- Before the presentation, familiarize yourself with the form to be used for that assignment. This will allow you to fill out a form easily and quickly during someone's speech.
- During the assigned speech, please be discreet while writing. You certainly don't want to distract the speaker! Keep your eyes on the speaker as much as possible so that you can accurately analyze the speaker's movement, eye contact, and other aspects of the speech.
- You may need to finish the form between other speeches, before you leave at the end of the class period, or even during other speeches. Again, discretion please! Add as much detail as possible.
- In the case of absence, peer critiques cannot be made up at a later date. Missed critiques will result in the assignment of 0 participation points.

Speaker Name _____

Instructor Feedback Summary – Nonfiction Narrative Speech
On your speaking day, attach this form to your presentation plan. Submit to your instructor before your speech.

I. Presentation Plan
- Complete
- Correct keyword outline form

II. Speech Development – Specific notes on back
- Meaningful focus
- Depth of critical thinking
- Logic of organization
- Richness of detail
- Other?

III. Speech Presentation – Specific notes on back
- Time
- Energy
- Preparedness
- Efficacy
- Other?

Grade _____

Note: Feedback on your speech --
　　　After you have turned in the required self-evaluation, your instructor will review the speech critiques from your peers and give them to you with your returned outline. As you review the instructor and peer critiques, look for the suggestions that are common among your reviewers. If you want help identifying those common threads to evaluate your own performance, please see your instructor.

Narrative Speech – Instructor Critique   **Speaker** _____

Unsatisfactory/Missing; Competent, Good, Excellent   **Notes**

Competencies		U	C	G	E
1. Topic/Audience	Chooses and narrows a topic appropriate for audience and occasion				
2. Thesis/Specific Purpose	Communicates an appropriate thesis/specific purpose				
3. Support	Provides appropriate supporting material, including vivid, sensory details				
	Develops appropriate presentation aids – selects object to enhance message				
4. Organization: 4a. Intro	Effective attention getter				
	Relates topic to audience				
	Relates topic to self (credibility); Reveals autobiographical significance				
	Clear and overt preview and/or mood setting				
4b. Body	Uses chronological order for narrative				
	Uses effective transitions and signposts				
4c. Conclusion	Effective closure				
5. Language	Uses appropriate language for designated audience				
6. Vocal Variety	Uses vocal variety in rate, pitch and intensity to heighten and maintain interest; appropriate energy/enthusiasm				
7. Vocal Accuracy	Uses appropriate pronunciation, grammar, & articulation.				
8. Physical Behaviors	Assertive stance; dressed appropriately				
	Uses movement and gestures effectively				
	Uses facial expressiveness and eye contact to support the message and engage with listeners				
	Effectively presents presentation aid to enhance message				
	Effectively uses note cards to support speech				

Speaker's time? _____

Strengths?

Areas for improvement?

Unit II Individual Research Project (IRP Part 1) -- Informative Oral Report

Overview: This unit will help you to build skills so that you can conduct research and document your work to meet the requirements of more than one assignment, including a research paper and a documented oral presentation (Units II and III).

Project components:

_____ **Part 1. Initial Plan --Appropriate Topic and MAP**

- Researchable, interesting, meaningful, based on personal expertise/interest
- Appropriate for assignments in Units II and III
- Identification of preliminary message, audience, and purpose

_____ **Part 2. Audience Analysis**
- Memo content -- Meaningful attention to required components
- Memo presentation -- Writing organization, format style and accuracy

_____ **Part 3. Research and Documentation**

- Appropriate selection of supporting materials -- current, varied, sufficient, credible
- Accurate documentation -- oral citations, bibliography
- Copies of quoted or paraphrased materials (as specified by instructor)

_____ **Part 4. a Oral Presentation**

- Content -- MAP, connection to audience, organization
- Delivery -- Eye contact, gestures, movement; oral citations; Q&A
- Presentation plan, drafts, preliminary work

Other requirements :
   Reading Assignments – See Syllabus and Canvas for text references and assigned essays.
   Unit II Quiz grade – WM, EC, sample informative essays and speeches
   Peer Critiques -- You earn participation points for each assigned peer critique.

Note: As you consider your focus for this oral report, be sure to keep in mind that you'll use the same topic for the next unit, a persuasive written report. While the paper and speech have the same topic, each will have a different focus regarding that topic.

COMM 1016 Course Guide   42

Goals
As you complete this unit, you will
- practice audience analysis and recognize differences between listeners and readers
- review and practice memo format
- develop expertise informative strategies
- enhance skills in gathering information (including use of databases)
- consider ethical approaches to managing information
- explore and experiment with the use of PowerPoint
- practice bibliography and oral citation formats
- practice strategies for handling audience questions
- develop increasing expertise with delivery techniques in individual presentations
- enhance skill with correct and effective writing of outlines

Presentation Requirements
Research, develop and present an informative speech based on your research. Across two units, you will be exploring a problem and solutions to that problem. Individuals will research, develop and present an informative speech on a meaningful and appropriately narrowed topic. Problem-solution design is frequently used in writing and speaking.

The best Individual Research Projects (IRPs) are based on problems that students already know about – problems in their families, neighborhoods, schools, or majors. For this unit, you will be presenting a documented speech to inform your audience about the problem. For the next unit, you will be writing a documented paper about the potential solutions to the problem.

Topics must be discussed with the instructor at some point during the planning process.

Your speech will be followed by a brief question-and-answer session-- the kind of experience likely to follow such a speech if you presented it to an academic committee or to colleagues in the workplace.

Topic: Problem that affects you and your audience – based on your prior knowledge and interest

Research: minimum of 4 cited sources

Writing

    Brainstorming/freewriting to develop content

    Audience analysis

    Research and interview notes (include use of database)

    Oral presentation plan; presentational aids including PowerPoint

    ~~**Bibliography**~~ **References page** of cited sources

Speaking -- Individual informative speech

    Length: 7-9 MINUTES, including question-and-answer session

    Presentational aids: PowerPoint <u>required</u>; additional use of audio, video, and/or objects should be kept to a minimum

Planning Your Presentation -- Checklist

Topic

_____Are you an expert? Try to choose a problem from your own experience so that you can build on your credibility with your audience.

_____Is your topic tied to a problem about which there are several potential solutions?

_____Has the topic been narrowed sufficiently so that you can address it **in detail** in the speech and later in the paper? Is your topic the equivalent of a chapter in a book? A whole book? Or a shelf in the library? (Choose something equivalent to "recycling in my dorm" instead of "world-wide pollution.")

MAP Decisions - Message

_____How will your specific topic translate into a message for your audience?

_____Will your message spark new thinking on the part of your audience?
(The might already be aware of the problem, but you might have new information or a new perspective. Don't tell them what they already know!)

MAP Decisions - Audience (not necessarily our class of first-year college students at VT).
Consider all of the various stakeholders before choosing one group.

_____Have you identified an audience who needs information and who would be interested in the problem and solutions?

_____Have you reviewed the strategies for a hostile, neutral or friendly audience?

_____Have you selected a specific audience who has interest in or control over the situation?

MAP Decisions - Purpose (General purpose - to inform)

_____What is the specific purpose of your presentation?

_____What level of information will your audience need?

Unit II, Part 2 -- Audience Analysis

Once you've chosen a topic, determine the identities of the "players" or stakeholders in this situation. Consider this audience as readers of your paper and listeners when you give your speech. For example, you want to give a speech about your involvement with the local animal shelter, you've identified a specific problem, and you've decided on a focus for your speech. You might choose an audience of (1) current shelter volunteers, (2) shelter administrators, (3) Virginia Tech students who might volunteer (4) local legislators who might have zoning authority, (5) state legislators who have funding authority, or (6) potential pet owners.

As you decide which of those audiences you might approach, you might consider numerous factors, including any of the following:
- With which group might you have the most credibility?
- Which group might be most hostile?
- Which group needs the most education?

Once you choose a group of stakeholders, consider the following questions:
- What do they have in common -- background, interests, education, geography, etc.?
- What do they care about?
- What do they need?
- What level of awareness do they have about your topic?

In a one-page memo, describe the group you'll address. (See the discussion of audience analysis in your text.) You may simply list their characteristics. Describe your connection with this group and the credibility you might have with them as you inform them about the problem. Our class will pretend to be that group when you give your speech.

Audience Analysis Memo -- Format and Content

The memo you write should include a standard memo heading and might include any of the information listed here. You might use these questions as a starting point to develop your audience analysis.

TO: Instructor's Name
FROM: Student's Name
DATE:
SUBJECT: Audience Analysis for Informative Report about _____

Parag 1 -- Audience identity -- Describe the audience and their connection to your topic. Why are they stakeholders? What problem do they face that is related to your topic? What do they need? (Maslow!) What is the attitude of the audience? Will they be neutral, friendly or hostile?

Parag 2 -- Key audience information (See your text) -- What demographic information or other specifics do you know about your audience? Age? Socio-economic background? Education? Experience with your topic?

Parag 3 -- Strategies -- How will you get the audience to "own" this problem? How will you build credibility with them? What kinds of resources will impress them?

Unit II, Part 3 -- Research Strategies and Documentation

Gathering Information
1. Your freewriting should list any information that you already know about the project. Be sure to keep of record of this prior knowledge so that you don't get confused later when you're trying to figure out where you found specific information.
2. Do a quick search for information found in the library collection and in the library databases.
3. Consider any primary sources you might develop. Is there someone you should interview? Is there a group of people you should survey? Virginia Tech has faculty who are experts at almost every subject! Interview one of them. If your topic is related to your community at home, interview a City Council member or a school principal. (Your instructor may require at least one interview.)
4. Are there websites with information relevant to your topic?
5. If you want to simply Google your topic, try Google Scholar (www.scholar.google.com) for sources that might have more validity than those you would find in a more generic Google search.

(**Note about Google**: Google works for an overview, but your project requires an in-depth look at a problem, not an overview. There is also no vetting of the sources provided. Using the library databases offers you more confidence that the sources have been peer reviewed or are reliable in some other way.)

Preparing a ~~Working Bibliography~~ References Page   4 sources → properly reference

As you are creating a working bibliography, you are simply collecting sources, not necessarily choosing sources that you will eventually use in the paper. Be sure to include a variety of types of current sources, including samples from the following:

- Sites found via internet search engines -- Use organizational websites, such as Red Cross, rather than personal websites, the validity of which may be hard to determine.
- Articles from databases (such as LexisNexis and other credible databases)
- Books
- Newspapers (not found via a database) -- perhaps your hometown paper if that's relevant
- Surveys and interviews

(Note: General encyclopedias—including Wikipedia--are not useful in college-level research except as a starting point for preliminary reading.)

Your working bibliography should be submitted in correct APA format to your instructor. This is good opportunity for you to ask questions and/or get some feedback on your format or selections.

Selecting Sources to Match MAP

As you sort through your information, you may be prompted to further narrow your topic and/or your audience. Since you'll be citing only a limited number of sources, you should consider your audience as you make those choices. What sources will be credible to your readers and listeners? What sources offer the best information on a particular topic?

<u>Evaluate carefully</u>! Are your sources varied? current? sufficient? credible?

Finalizing the Bibliography
Your final bibliography will be a pared-down version of the working bibliography. You will submit a version of the bibliography with your paper, and another version with your speech.

Unit II, Part 4 – Organization and Delivery

Meeting Audience Needs
For your research project, you chose an audience who had some connection with the topic. They are stakeholders who care – or should care – about the problem and the solution.

The readers who read your written report will have the luxury of re-reading a paragraph or examining closely a visual you include that supports your text. They could take their time to be sure they understood. Readers might even look at some of your sources online or make notes about questions. They might read your paper while they drink coffee, listen to music, or in other ways control the environment.

Listeners, on the other hand, have fewer options and much less time to absorb the ideas you're presenting. As you develop this speech, consider their needs for information <u>and</u> the situation in which they'll be hearing your speech. They may be physically uncomfortable, or they may be distracted by other people in the room. You need to do everything you can to engage them, keep their attention, and help them to capture the information.

Organizing for Listeners
Your readers didn't need for you to repeat the main points, but your listeners do. The intro should preview the main ideas, the body should include explanations of ideas, and the conclusion should have a summary. Try to help the listener learn and remember the main points.

Organize the solutions using one of the patterns in your text. You might use a topical pattern (or even chronological order) to prove that the problem exists and that is important to the reader. That is, your paper would focus on a definition and analysis of the problem. Choose an organizational pattern that will help your listeners absorb the information.

Note: Historical approaches (chronological order) to a problem may seem easier for a speaker, but they may bore a reader. If you choose that approach, you have a bigger challenge in engaging the reader.

Use repeated phrases and/or transitions to help readers know that you're moving from point to point or to understand the ways in which the ideas are connected.

Build a credible argument; prove that the problem exists and that your readers are involved. Be sure to balance ethos, logos, and pathos. Your listeners will be bored by a speech that is all data and no humanity; they will be suspicious of a speech that is all human interest and no data. They also need to recognize YOUR credibility as a speaker. How are you personally connected to this problem?

Presentation Techniques for Listeners
A paper requires a standard format, appropriate language choice, correct spelling and grammar, well crafted sentences, and accurate APA documentation.

Your oral presentation depends on your live delivery of the information, still requiring attention to the components listed for the written presentation. Additionally, your nonverbal communication, your vocal delivery, your management of note cards (4 x 6 with writing on one side only), and your oral citation of sources will all help your listeners understand and respect the information you're presenting.

Unit III Individual Research Project (IRP, Part 2) – Persuasive Written Report

Overview: This project will allow you to build on your work in Unit II. Much of the preliminary work has already been accomplished, and now you will shift to persuading your audience about possible solutions to the problem you researched.

_____ **Audience analysis** (revised as necessary from Unit II)

Content -- Meaningful attention to required components
Delivery -- Writing organization, format style and accuracy

_____ **Research** (revised from Unit II)

Appropriate selection of supporting materials -- current, varied, sufficient, credible
Seamless integration into presentations
Accurate documentation -- parenthetical citations, bibliography
Copies of quoted or paraphrased materials (as specified by instructor)

_____ **Persuasive Written Report** -- Solutions

- Brainstorming/freewriting to develop content
- Logical organization to meet readers' needs; use of accurate outline form
- Content – MAP: connection to audience needs; developed with rich, credible and appropriate information; effective argument
- Presentation -- Format, style, accuracy, visual representation of data

Other requirements :

Reading assignments: See Syllabus and Canvas for text references and assigned essays.
Unit III Quiz– *Writing Matters, Understanding Human Communication*, essays
Peer reviews of written work - You earn participation points for each peer review.

Goals

As you complete this unit, you will
- practice audience analysis and recognize differences between listeners and readers
- develop expertise with argument and designs for persuasive presentations
- practice bibliography and parenthetical citation formats
- develop increasing expertise with APA formatting and documentation
- practice integration of quotes into text
- enhance skill with correct and effective writing
- consider ethical approaches to persuasion

[handwritten notes: strategies for speech/paper → one page self-reflection on everything; 1. new audience analysis; 2. new interview; 3. outline for paper April 11th, upload to canvas. Final → 16th.]

Presentation Requirements

Research, develop and present a persuasive written report based on the research from Unit II. Because persuasion often includes information, you would explain solutions and give data about their potential for solving the problem. Develop sound arguments; prove that these solutions are viable. Recommend a solution for your readers to adopt.

You might be discussing questions of fact, value or policy as noted in your text. You'll be using argument to persuade your audience, and you'll be including ethos, logos and pathos.

This assignment requires an in-depth look at the solutions, not an overview, not the equivalent of an encyclopedia article!

This is the kind of research you might be asked to conduct at an internship or in your career when a group or administrator is trying to make a decision about a course of action. You might be asked to do the research about the existence or feasibility of solutions to a problem.

Topic: Solutions to a problem about which you have some prior knowledge and interest

Research: minimum of 4 cited sources

Writing
- ***Audience analysis** -- revised if necessary from Unit II
- ***Research and interview notes** (include use of database) -- revised if necessary from Unit II (*If no revision is necessary, your instructor may require only the outline and the revised bibliography.)
- **Outline** and evidence of other steps in the writing process
- **Persuasive Written report (research paper)** based on solutions to a problem, including **Bibliography** -- Your paper should follow a standard APA format, with appropriate language choice, correct spelling and grammar, well crafted sentences, and accurate documentation. Your instructor may require that a 1-page outline be provided in place of the abstract.
- **Self-evaluation of entire IRP** – In a one-page memo, discuss your successes and challenges with topic selection, research, project planning, oral presentation, and/or written presentation. Include your strategies for meeting needs of listeners and readers.

Developing and Presenting the Written Report

Readers vs. Listeners -- While the topic of your oral presentation and your written presentation are the same for Units II and III, be careful that you recognize the different needs of readers and listeners.

The listeners to your speech appreciated your pointing out the structure of the speech with a preview and overt listing and repeating of main points. The "ministerial three" was obvious.

Readers don't need repetition; in fact, they get bored with it. They don't need a listing of main points in the thesis and the conclusion. They'll actually feel insulted if you keep repeating the same points. They appreciate an intro that suggests what's to come--one that invites the reader to read further, not one that gives up all the surprises.

Process
   Writing Process -- Follow the steps of writing process that we have discussed in class: freewriting, gathering information, outlining, drafting, editing, and proofreading. Due dates for those steps will be provided by your instructor.
   Organization -- To explain the solutions related to your topic, use a standard design. See the description in your text of problem-solution design, and refer to any articles assigned.
   Peer Review – Ask a classmate (or two) to review your rough draft. Your instructor may provide workshop time in class for you to complete the Writing Workshop form.

Organization -- Because the paper should engage your readers, be careful to capture their interest. Use a blend of data and human interest or narrative. Remember – logos, pathos, ethos!

Your paper will focus only on the possible solutions to the problem. The solutions might be presented from least to most expensive or in some other logical order. You might want to begin with a solution that involves no change and end with the solution that is your preferred solution. Your outline might follow this pattern:
   I.   Review of problem
   II. Solution 1
   III. Solution 2
   IV. Solution 3

Outline Details -- As you analyze the problem for your written report, you might use some variation of the following outline to organize your report. Your instructor will provide more specific information about the required outline. You will include at least the following components:
   1. Tentative title -- a phrase that will intrigue your reader and suggest the paper's focus
   2. MAP decisions
      M: What is the main idea that you want the paper to convey to your readers?
      A: Specific group to whom your paper is addressed
      P: To persuade the readers about what?
   3. Tentative thesis -- a sentence that will suggest the focus of the paper and include a suggestion about the writer's position or attitude
   4. Outline of main points to be covered in the body of the essay; use Roman numerals for this section and keyword phrases for this section. Develop the outline to at least the A, B, C level with each Roman numeral.
   5. Conclusion-- a sentence indicating your plan for the conclusion.

From Outline to Draft
Be sure that the bones of your outline are visible to readers as they read your draft. Your organizational signals will help them move through your paper.

Intro -- They'll be looking for a thesis statement in the intro paragraph, usually at the end of that paragraph. Readers of a short paper don't need to read a list of the main points in the thesis, then again in the body, then again in the conclusion. Give them a peek into the main focus of the paper. Set the tone.

Since you will be balancing logos, pathos, and ethos in your paper–just as you did in your speech–you might consider opening with pathos, something to put a human face on the problem or solution.

Body -- Sections should have headings (as shown in APA style), but the headings don't replace the need for topic sentences in body paragraphs. Those topic sentences should show the focus of the paragraph and should be followed by solid arguments, proving the existence and extent of the problem. Specific evidence should be cited; visuals should be included to help readers understand data.

Readers also need transitions as you move from idea to idea at the beginning of body paragraphs and within paragraphs.

Conclusion -- The conclusion can't introduce an idea or simply repeat the main points. The conclusion needs to be as engaging as the introduction. You've carefully moved the readers to this point in the paper; now you might remind readers of their connection to the problem. Give them something to think about. They'll remember most what they read last.

Format
Carefully follow the format in *Writing Matters*, including the use of a page header and page numbers. The sample paper is annotated to explain various aspects of formatting.

Title page – The title should engage your reader, not merely name the assignment
Body of paper -- Use format described shown in the text.
(Your instructor may require a 1-page outline in place of the abstract.)
- Use centered headings for various sections.
- Use parenthetical citation to document sources (APA style).
- Check the relationship of parenthetical citation to the bibliography. Usually, the first word in the bibliography entry is the word used in the parenthetical citation.
- Check the thesis statement, topic sentences, and transitions.
- Use tables and graphs as appropriate. (Minimum of on visual is required.)
- Revise and edit with care!

Bibliography – The bibliography (APA style) should list only those sources that are cited in the paper. The bibliography must include a variety of types of current sources.

Submission of final draft
When you turn in your final draft (stapled or bound), please submit the following:
- one final draft of the researched report, including title page and bibliography
- copy of feedback form
- one rough draft of entire paper
- one keyword outline of entire paper (either as part of your writing process or substituted for the abstract – check with your instructor)
- all other preliminary work, including personal research notes and/or a copy of the first page of any article you used as a resource (Check with your instructor.)

Unit IV Persuasive Group Presentation

Overview: The persuasive presentation will be developed and presented by various groups as they explore local issues and seek future involvement from the audience.

Group Grade

_____ Proposal -- content/organization, format, style, accuracy

_____ Presentation Plan and Bibliography
- Appropriate selection of supporting materials -- current, varied, sufficient, credible
- Effective integration into presentations
- Accurate documentation -- bibliography

_____ Oral Presentation -- seamlessness of presentation, effective organization, consistent visuals, overall content & delivery

Individual Grade

_____ Group interaction and contribution -- attendance, cooperation, fulfilling assigned roles, communication with members, consistent and effective contributions (Provide evidence of contributions and research.)

_____ Oral presentation -- content and delivery of individual section, references to sources (oral citations), attentiveness to others

_____ Self-evaluation – informal consideration of personal and group strengths and areas for improvement

Other requirements :
Reading Assignments – See Syllabus and Canvas for text references and assigned essays.
Peer Critiques - You earn participation points for each assigned peer critique.

Unit IV Quiz– *Writing Matters, Understanding Human Communication,* essays

---

Consider this resource at Lynda.com – "Effective Meetings"
http://www.lynda.com/Business-Collaboration-tutorials/Effective-Meetings/81262-2.html

Goals

As you complete this unit, you will
- enhance skill with persuasive speech designs
- develop research skills including use of library, net searches, and interviews
- practice audience analysis
- examine and practice proposal format
- practice building a bibliography
- practice cooperative learning and team presentation skills
- enhance skill with correct and effective writing
- consider ethical approaches to providing information and persuading an audience
- practice Monroe's Motivated Sequence
- explore and experiment with the use of PowerPoint

Presentation Requirements
- Presentation goal -- Persuasive Group Presentation
- Length of oral presentation: 20-30 minutes
- Presentational aids: 1 per person (minimum)
- Research: 3 cited sources per person (minimum)
- Related Writing:
    - **Group proposal** --2-4 pages (developed by group)
    - **Presentation plan or outline** (developed by group)
    - Notes from research (including library and database search) and interview/survey (collected by individuals, analyzed by group, submitted by individuals)
    - **Bibliography** of cited sources (developed by group)
    - **Self-evaluation** – Informal writing (developed by individuals)

Creating a Researched Presentation

This presentation should be a group effort. While individual members might contribute information for particular sections, the group must work together to create an intro, a conclusion, transitions from speaker to speaker, and a bibliography. First, you will begin meeting in groups to assign roles, select a topic, and to make your MAP decisions.

Topic: Campus or Community Resources

Campus resources – As a valuable service to the class or to another designated audience, your group members would explore the services offered by a particular campus organization. You would determine who can use the services, where they are located, what hours they're available, and the ways in which people can get more information or can register for assistance. Of course, the components of the presentations will vary depending on the campus resource selected. Your group will make those specific decisions later. You might present your information to a class of freshman college students who are not familiar with that particular office and may need to take advantage of such a service. Since persuasion always includes some information, you will inform your audience about the service or organization and then encourage them to participate – to attend, to contribute, or to support.

Community resources for promoting cross-cultural exchange and support -- Some CommSkills classes will engage in service learning this semester. They will volunteer as a group, research the problems faced by a particular population in the community, and present their information to a specific audience who might be (1) involved with this project or (2) willing to help with such work in the future. Components of this project will be adapted to meet the needs of groups who are participating in this service learning opportunity.

Group Meeting #1

Housekeeping
Introduce yourselves, make a list of group members, and decide on a name for your group. (Make notes below.) Check to be sure that each of you has contact information for each group member. Do not use the class listserv to send messages that apply only to your group members. Ask someone in your group to take notes today only.

Group interaction
You studied information about group behaviors last semester, and you're reading the rest of that text material this semester. From this very first group meeting, pay attention to careful verbal and nonverbal communication. Be a valuable contributor to your group – not a dominator, not a slacker. Include all group members in decision-making; ask for input if necessary.

Topic possibilities
Brainstorm a list of campus resources. Consider offices you have visited on campus and programs you have heard about. As you brainstorm with the group, try to avoid evaluating the ideas; instead, develop a rich list from which you can make a choice at the next meeting.

Preparing for Group Meeting #2
Consider tasks to be accomplished before the next meeting. Individuals should agree to add topics to the brainstormed list before the next meeting. Group members might check the VT website or discuss possibilities with roommates, other classmates, and/or faculty. At the second meeting, you will decide on a specific topic, assign group roles, and plan specific research tasks.

Ask someone to begin the collection of paperwork generated by the group; initial, date and save today's brainstorming. Ask someone to send a message to the entire group (include your instructor) about today's meeting.

Group name:

Group members and contact info:

Top topic possibilities (after brainstorming and in-class discussion):

Group Meeting #2 -- Roles and Topic

1. Determine the roles for all members of your group. These roles serve to coordinate the work of ALL members in the group. The roles listed below might be reconfigured to fit the size or of the group. Fill in the blanks on this page for your reference.

2. Next decide on the topic for your group and also begin to focus on research possibilities. Review to the criteria for the assignment and consider the information on the following page about topic selection. Be sure to reach consensus in your group about the topic!

Group name_____   Specific topic _____

Logistics and Communication Director   _____

This person should help schedule meeting times and places, record notes from each meeting, send e-mail to group members and the instructor, and handle other physical arrangements. This person should schedule a CommLab appointment and also serve as the liaison with the instructor. The notes from each in-class or out-of-class meeting should include the following information: group members present, length of meeting, tasks accomplished, assignments for the next meeting, and plan for next meeting.

Time Manager and Proposal Director   _____

First, this person should lead the group's work on the proposal. With input from the whole group, this person should then create a timeline for research and preparation, based on the due dates for the panel presentation and the written presentation. Copies of the timeline should be distributed to all members. This person should also provide time cues to the group during informal and formal discussions.

Research Director: _____

This person should orchestrate the research of the groups so that all requirements are met efficiently. This person might also compile data collected by various group members into a chart. Eventually this person will collect bibliography entries (submitted in correct form) from each group member; he or she will alphabetize the entries and create the reference list for the report. All group members will review the bibliography and assist with editing.

Oral Presentation Director and Functional Leader: _____

This person should direct the presentation (oversee the organization and presentation plan) and prepare a brief intro and conclusion. (Your group might decide to assign the conclusion to the person who presents the last part of the panel.)

Manager of Visuals; Audience Analysis Director   _____

First, this person should also direct the preparation of the audience analysis, which is part of the proposal. Then this person should consider appearances. For the presentation, he or she should foster a discussion of "wardrobe," coordinate presentational aids, and check arrangement of chairs and equipment. This person should also prepare consistent graphics for the written presentation.

Note: Outlines for Group Meetings #1 and #2 are provided in this *Course Guide* because they have predictable and essential components. Subsequent meetings will vary and will be orchestrated by each group's members.

Selecting a Topic

First, review the criteria for this assignment, and then review the brainstormed list your group generated at the prior meeting.

Second, ask for any addition for the list. What campus resources did group members find after the last meeting?

Next, evaluate the ideas on your brainstormed list. Your topic choice should be one that is of interest to all group members and fits the following criteria:

- Prior knowledge -- Because you probably have little prior knowledge of some campus resources, you might consider programs with which you have some familiarity or interest. You will become an expert by researching the topic thoroughly.
- In-depth focus -- Choose a topic that can be discussed in detail within the time allotted. Avoid an overview.
- Availability of sufficient, current, varied, reputable research -- Choose a researchable topic, one that can be supported with recent information.
- Freshness of focus --Select a topic that will provide new and useful ideas to your audience or will cause your audience to see a familiar topic in a new way.
- Current/future usefulness – Choose a topic that will be useful to your designated audience – maybe VT students at Orientation, 2nd semester students at a dorm meeting, new members of a campus major or club.

Once your topic is approved by your instructor, you might move on to discussion of research or deadlines. (See the following pages in this *Course Guide* for more information about resource selection and timeline establishment.) After you finish your research, you will be able to narrow your topic and make a decision about your focus or message.

Research - Collecting and Choosing Sources

To collect supporting materials for your topic, consider the many resources, including yourselves, that are available on campus and in the library databases. Explore the following possibilities:

- Pool the expertise of the group concerning your topic.
- Use library resources to expand your information. The class will spend one class period in the library with some brief instruction from a librarian.
- Use the library for books and periodicals that are not available online.
- Use online resources related to your topic. The class will discuss and determine criteria for the use of net resources.

Research -- Explore the library site for further information:
Virginia Tech's Library - http://www.lib.vt.edu/
    Library Virtual tour
    Research
    Citation and Style manuals

Use of Interviews and Surveys

Interviews. Your group may decide to interview an expert, a faculty advisor or professor who is involved with the subject you're researching. Such an interview would be included in your bibliography; it should be documented and verifiable. The goal of an interview is for you to get information in a conversational setting from an expert. Interviewing is an interpersonal skill that you must continue to develop all through your college career. Of course, submitting questions via e-mail does not fill the requirements of the interview as discussed in your text.

The interview process: If you interview an expert, use the interview process outlined below.
- Brainstorm a list of potential interviewees with your group. Discuss the possibilities; check with your instructor if you have questions about identifying a candidate.
- The group should suggest questions for the interview as the interview plan is developed. A list of questions should be developed.
- Make an appointment and promise a specified length for the interview.
- Be familiar with the topic, having conducted at least minimal research, before the interview.
- Conduct an organized interview so that all points can be covered during the time allotted.
- Take notes and add them to the other research notes collected for the project.
- Send a thank-you note after your interview. (You may email this note with a copy to your instructor.) Your instructor may also contact the interviewee to thank him or her for participating.

Surveys. Use a survey when you want to find out the opinions of those who may or may not be familiar with a subject; they are not experts. Surveys are often used when you're trying to find out how much people know about a certain topic or how satisfied they are with a certain situation. A survey can be used as a citation if at least a dozen students are polled, preferably more.

Usually if a group uses a survey, every member of the group helps to create the survey and then conducts the survey with a certain number of people. Then the group pools and analyzes the responses. With that procedure, the responses will come from a greater variety of people. Individual group members should provide evidence of the use of surveys and any analysis when submitting copies of other research. The more people you survey, the more reliable your data will be.

Caution: When you analyze survey responses, take care to focus on the average response. Don't generalize from one person's experience. Always acknowledge that your pool of participants is not representative of all the students involved. Be sure that your presentations include some description of the survey procedure and results (number of people polled, kinds of questions, general responses).

Creating a Timeline

Due dates for certain components of this group assignment will be determined by your instructor. However, many tasks need to be completed, and the group members should agree on a timeframe for all group and individual activities. Use this chart as a guide for discussion.

Below is a partial list of project components. Your group will want to add other tasks and determine dates for their completion. Although the list is linear, certain activities will occur along with other activities. For example, research will begin while the proposal is being written. Communicating these dates to each other AND being responsible for them will certainly enhance the success of your group. Your timer can finalize and distribute a list of dates for the group.

Partial list of project components	Due Date
Topic choice and group roles – provide list to instructor	
Proposal	
• determination of responsibility for sections of proposal	
• audience analysis ready for group review	
• other sections prepared for incorporation into draft	
• draft ready for group editing	
• *final draft due to instructor (in time for useful feedback on project)*	
Research	
• determination of responsibility for researching various sources	
• surveys and/or interviews planned, conducted, analyzed	
• sharing of research among the group	
• *individual bibliographies due to Research Director and to instructor*	
• group bibliography ready for group review and editing	
• *group bibliography due to instructor*	
Presentation Plan and Visuals	
• decision-making about MAP, strategies for the presentation, visuals	
• *individual outlines due to instructor Oral Presentation Director*	
• draft of presentation plan ready for group review	
• individual visuals ready	
Rehearsal -- CommLab?	
Presentation -- *group's presentation plan and bibliog. due*	

Persuasive Presentation Proposal

Once you have completed your brainstorming for a topic, your preliminary research, and your reading about speech design, you will submit a proposal concerning your researched speeches. The proposal format is often used to request approval and/or funding for a project, so the process is important for you to master. Professionals write proposals routinely when they seek grant funding, project approval, or budget authorizations.

Use the following format for a typed proposal (2-4 pages); convince your instructor that your plan is a good one. Be sure that the proposal is submitted in time so that your instructor can give you good feedback before you finalize your group presentation.

Steps in Completing the Group's Proposal

1. Through a series of activities--such as brainstorming for a topic, reviewing speech designs, and beginning your research--make important decisions **as a group** about your researched speech. Create a MAP and organize your proposal.

2. Type a rough draft of a proposal using line spacing as assigned and the following headings:

- **Memo heading** -- Use memo form
- **Introduction** -- Statement of proposal: topic, audience
- **Audience Need** – Why is this presentation necessary? Why does the audience need this information?
- **Recommendation** -- How will your choice of topic, audience, and sources be the best for the situation?
- **Supplementary Materials** -- List the sources you'll use to support your speech.
- **Conclusion** -- In a brief paragraph, "sell" your idea. You might comment on the plan's benefits or its feasibility.

3. Edit (for accuracy and style) and proofread. All group members should contribute to and review the draft and final; the group's proposal coordinator is not solely responsible for this work.

4. Attach a list of questions your group has decided to use in an interview. Provide the name of the interviewee and the date of the proposed interview.

Usage note: *As you create the parts of this project, please review the spelling and usage of "freshman" and "freshmen." The first is singular; the second is plural. Try substituting the word "senior" or "seniors" in your sentence, and then you'll know if you should use singular or plural.*

Sample Format for Proposal (single-space or line and a half)

TO: (name of instructor)

FROM: The _____ Group (list names of all group members)

DATE: _____

SUBJECT: Persuasive Presentation Proposal

Introduction

Use a few sentences to explain why your topic is an important one. Mention the narrowed topic and the audience. Conclude this paragraph with a thesis statement referring to the focus of this document.

Audience Need

Begin this section with a topic sentence explaining the focus of this section. Why should your group make this presentation? Why does your audience need the information you plan to present? (Consider Maslow.) Who are they? (Include an audience analysis: audience type, audience purpose, demographics, attitudes, beliefs, and values.) How are they connected to this issue? How much do they already know about the issue? How will they benefit from knowing more about this issue? What will you challenge them to do?

Recommendation

Begin this section with a topic sentence explaining the focus of this section. Recommend an approach that will meet the needs of your audience. Explain the types of research materials you will consider. In a second paragraph, comment on your process (responsibilities and timeframe). Explain which group members will undertake which components of the presentation.

Supplementary Materials

Begin this section with a topic sentence explaining the focus of this section. Use specific detail to describe the facilities, supplies, and other resources you'll use for your project. Include costs where appropriate.

Conclusion

Use this final paragraph to wrap up your proposal. Convince your reader that your presentation will successfully meet the needs of your audience. Comment on the feasibility of your group's process.

Bibliography

One bibliography of all cited sources will be submitted by each group. The materials shown on the reference list should be recent and should include ONLY those references you will cite in your presentation. The bibliography must include a variety of current sources: at least one interview, at least one journal article referencing other campuses, at least one book (perhaps about trends/approaches at other institutions), and any other pamphlets, newspaper or magazine articles, reputable web sources, etc. Do not attempt to create a reading list.

Process -- Each group member will collect his or her sources, and submit a list of correctly formatted sources to the instructor and to the group's research coordinator. The research coordinator will create a master list of references and will share copies with all group members for editing purposes. Group members should submit corrections in a timely manner so that the research director has adequate time to prepare the final copy.

The bibliography will be turned in with your speech plan on the day of your presentation.

Format -- We will review APA style in class. Rely on your handbook and any websites your instructor may suggest. The library site maintains an updated section on "Citation and Style Manuals."

To set up each line of the bibliography, use the "hanging indent" command in Word. (Click on "format" and then "paragraph" and then "special.") With the use of this command, the first line of each entry will begin at the margin and subsequent lines will be indented.

Oral Presentation

The group presentation will consist of various presenters who each cover a main idea related to the selected topic. Each member should provide in-depth information about your topic so that your audience members will understand its importance/usefulness to their own lives.

Development of content – As a group member, you will research, develop and present one section of the topic (as determined through the course of various group meetings). You should submit an outline draft to the instructor and to the oral presentation coordinator so that the coordinator can integrate the outlines and prepare a presentation plan. A draft of that plan should be reviewed by all group members so that a final copy will be ready by the day of the presentation.

Delivery goal -- Deliver a <u>seamless</u>, conversational team presentation with coordinated formats and visuals. Presenters will be seated in the front of the room, to the right or left side (facing the class). You will stand when it is your turn to present.

Use an extemporaneous delivery style; do not read or memorize your researched report.

All strategies for effective delivery apply to this presentation: eye contact, movement, vocal variety, facial expression, and effective use of note cards. Practice your delivery! Practice saying the sources from which you took information; include enough information so that your audience is impressed by the credibility of your sources. Practice transitions from one speaker to the next.

Organization – Use Monroe's Motivated Sequence. Look for MMS in advertising, letters to the editor, or sample persuasive essays – either those articles assigned for class or examples in *Writing Matters*. MMS is a classic organizational plan for persuasion.

Paperwork -- Please submit the following materials on the day of your group's presentation: (1) group's presentation plan; (2) bibliography (APA style), listing only those sources that will be cited during the presentation; and (3) critique sheet from each presenter with individual's name at top. (Note: Each presenter may be asked to turn in note cards and any handouts after the presentation.)

Presentation Plan

Complete one presentation plan for your entire group. All members should contribute to and review the plan. Attach a bibliography. The format shown here reflects Monroe's Motivated Sequence (MMS), used across the entire presentation. Groups also might consider having each person use a shortened form of MMS for each segment of the speech. Check with your instructor about ways to adapt this or other persuasive strategies.

Group members: (list all names)
Topic:
MAP:
I. Introduction *(MMS Attention)*
- Attention-getting strategy
- Credibility statement
- Connection with audience needs (audience interest, benefit)
- Focus and/or preview statement (While a preview statement is found only in the introduction, a focus statement might be used later in the speech.)
- (You might include introduction of all group members early in the introduction or as part of the preview.)

II. _____ *(MMS Need -- Problem)*
Mini-intro
A. Explain the problem and its connection to audience needs
B. Provide data to prove the problem exists
C. etc. (Amount of information necessary will depend on audience's familiarity with the subject.)
Mini-conclusion and transition to next speaker

III. _____ *(MMS Satisfaction – Solution)*
Mini-intro
A. Explain the solution you recommend
B. Provide evidence to prove that this solution is the best or is workable
Mini-conclusion and transition to next speaker

IV. _____ *(MMS Visualization-- Future)*
Mini-intro
A. Explain what the future will be like if the solution is or is not implemented.
B. Use vivid details and emotional appeal
Mini-conclusion and transition to next speaker

V. _____ *(MMS Action -- Appeal for audience involvement to create change)*
Mini-intro
A. What can they do immediately?
B. What information do they need and where will they find it?
Mini-conclusion and transition to conclusion

Conclusion: See text for strategies; indicate approach on outline

(Reminder: Each presenter must <u>cite</u> three sources, use at least one visual, and may use 3-5 note cards.)

Rehearsal Notes for Group Project

Following is a list of tasks that you might use as you complete your preparations for the group project. This list is based on the assumption that you are familiar with all requirements as listed in the Course Guide and with the related reading material in *Writing Matters* and *Understanding Human Communication*. The list below is based on the description of roles in this *Course Guide*. Your group may have decided to redistribute these tasks based on the number of people in your group or other considerations. Your group may also ask member to perform other tasks that are not listed here. Add notes to these pages to reflect any changes in assignments.

Logistics and Communication Director --
- Help the group to schedule a final run-through of the entire presentation.
- Make an appointment at CommLab (commlab@vt.edu). If your group is having trouble finding time to meet within the times allotted, send email requesting an alternate time. The coaches **may** be able to schedule a special time for your group
- Other?

Research Director --
- Prepare final copy of the group's bibliography in time so that all members can review and edit. Follow format as shown in *Writing Matters*; see sample bibliography at the end of the sample research paper in the text.
- Help your group members practice citing their sources. Each group member should provide at least two important pieces of information to cite a source. If the audience might recognize an author or title, use either of those components of the citation along with the date (to emphasize currency of the source). For example, "According to *Time Magazine*, October 15, 2010, students love ice cream. . ." (In this case, the audience wouldn't recognize an author's name, so there's no need to include it.) "In *The Journal of Student Affairs*, Spring 2012, researchers indicated that . . . " (This lends credibility to the speech by noting a national journal with a current date.) "Bill Clinton, in his State of the Union address, January 1999, described . . . " (In this case, the audience would recognize the author of the quote, so the name should be included."
- Bring a copy of the final bibliography to class on the day that your group presents.
- Other?

Oral Presentation Director --
- Prepare a final copy of the group's presentation plan according to the example given in the *Course Guide*. Be sure that all group members have a chance to edit.
- Direct the group's rehearsal of the entire presentation. Be thoroughly familiar with all requirements so that you can help your group meet the expectation.
- Focus on the flow of the presentation with smooth transitions from speaker to speaker. The presentation should have fully integrated components; it shouldn't seem like a series of very separate speeches. If the group is using any themes or props to unify the presentation, be sure that the group members emphasize these components.
- Clip together all paperwork that should be turned in on the day of the presentation. Remind your group members that evidence of individual contributions will be submitted later with the self-evaluation.
- Other?

Manager of Visuals; Audience Analysis Director --
- Review with group members the standards for dress that all of you decided to follow.
- Arrange chairs and overhead for rehearsal and on the day of the presentation.
- Review all presentational aids to be sure they are consistent for all group members and meet basic guidelines (PowerPoint template, 6x6 rule, titles, etc.) If the group is offering any handouts, plan for the distribution of the handouts at the end of the entire presentation.
- Pay special attention to the relationship of the presentation to the audience analysis. Make sure that all information ties to the audience needs and heightens information relevance. Check the MAP.
- The group's use of note cards will also create a visual effect; offer reminders about effective use of note cards.
- Other?

Time Manager and Proposal Director --
- Be sure that the group has adhered to the promise of this project as outlined in the proposal. If significant changes are made, check with your instructor.
- Help the group meet the time requirements. Arrange a signal for group members who are speaking so that they know if they're close to a time limit.
- Other?

Individual Speakers --
- Review all assignment requirements.
- Check to be sure that your own parts of the group presentation include a mini-intro (tied to audience need), specific details in the body, and a mini-conclusion that may include the transition to the next speaker. Within your presentation, use strategies to connect points as noted in your text.
- Emphasize your own credibility with the research and your familiarity with this resource.
- Review your information in your text about delivery. Thoroughly prepare this extemporaneous speech (without memorizing it) and maintain a friendly and conversational style. Try for warmth and enthusiasm.
- Create note cards with large, bold key words. Practice using the note cards.
- **Introduction of entire presentation** -- Check requirements in Course Guide. Be sure to emphasize group's credibility and emphasize the importance of this presentation to your audience. Identify the audience in the intro -- such as, "As second-semester freshmen, you may not have had the chance to fully use this campus resource." "As incoming freshmen at VT, you will spend many hours at . . . " "Since you are just beginning your studies here, you will want to know about. . . "
- **Conclusion of the entire presentation** -- Provide some kind of wrap up, ask for questions, and save a final line or two for the final comment. Again, emphasize the ways in which this resource is important to your audience.
- Other?

Self-Evaluation

Consider the strengths and weaknesses of your group process. Provide a sense of the overall group performance, but focus most on your specific contributions to that performance. This is NOT an opportunity to attack those group members who may not have fulfilled their roles. However, you might indicate the points at which you may have had to make up for another member's lapse. Your instructor will determine the format of this self-evaluation.

You might consider any of the following as strengths or areas for improvement:

Group process - What formal or informal role did you play in the group process? Did you attend all the meetings? How did you support the group's effort? Could the group rely on you to show initiative and to follow through with the tasks you agreed to do? Were your contributions made in a timely manner?

Research -- How did you contribute to the group's research task? What worked and what didn't? How did you handle your obligation to contribute to the bibliography?
Oral presentation/Presentational aids - What was your contribution to the organization and rehearsal process? How did you contribute to the ideas for and creation of presentational aids? How effective were you on the day of the presentation? What would you change for next time?

Group presentation -- How effective was your interaction with the group during the final presentation? Did you appear interested in other speakers? How did you assist the group and its effort to make a cohesive presentation?

Group Persuasive Speech Critique   Group member:_____

Unsatisfactory/missing; Competent; Good; Excellent   Notes

Competencies		U	C	G	E
1. Topic/ Audience	Chooses and narrows a topic appropriate for audience and occasion.				
2. Thesis/ Specific Purpose	Communicates the thesis/specific purpose in a manner appropriate for audience/occasion				
3. Support	Provides adequate and credible supporting material appropriate for topic and audience				
	Uses effective and ethical argument				
	Effectively cites required number of sources (# cited? 1 2 3 more)				
	Incorporates balance of emotional and logical appeal				
	Develops effective PowerPoint to support (not repeat) speech.				
4. Organization:	Uses appropriate organizational pattern				
4a. Intro	Effective mini-intro to individual's portion of the presentation (attention-getter; thesis)				
4b. Body	Presents argument in logical sequence, appropriate for audience				
	Uses effective transitions within speech				
4c. Conclusion	Restates thesis; emphasizes call to action if appropriate				
	Concludes with impact and transitions to next speaker				
5. Language	Uses language that is appropriate to the audience, occasion & purpose.				
6. Vocal Variety	Uses vocal variety in rate, pitch & intensity to heighten audience interest; appropriate energy				
7. Vocal Accuracy	Uses pronunciation, grammar, & articulation				
8. Physical Behaviors	Uses assertive stance; dressed appropriately				
	Uses movement and gestures effectively				
	Uses facial expressiveness and eye contact to support the message and engage listeners				

Speaker's Time? _____

Group's overall effectiveness	Persuasive and likely to achieve goal with intended audience				
Group's message/ content	Meaningful, well organized, well supported; clear MAP				
Group's delivery	Energetic, attentive to group members and audience; well rehearsed; effective transitions				
Group's visual effectiveness	Coherent, appropriate, effective personal appearance and visuals				

Use reverse for further notes about speaker and/or group.

Critiqued by _____

Final – Collect, Reflect, Connect

A portfolio, reflection essay, and resume will be due at the end of the semester. During the final exam meeting, you will submit this work and will complete a final speaking activity. As you complete these final assignments, you will accomplish the following:
- practice analysis and reflection writing
- review format for standard essays and resumes
- enhance skill with correct and effective writing
- explore strategies for compiling, organizing and displaying work

1. Collect – Portfolio. Construct a portfolio of your work during this academic year. Your portfolio should be not only a collection of work, but also a useful reference for you in the future. In order to be useful, it must be organized in some logical fashion and must include any necessary labels to lead the reader (you or me) to its different sections. To create your portfolio --
   1. Collect all your work. Include all assignments, even preliminary drafts or outlines.
   2. Decide on a way to bind and organize the work. Add a table of contents, using some symbol (such as a star) to mark the three best assignments! Add any other organizers (explanations or "road signs") for readers of your portfolio.
   3. Add the work to your collection from the first semester and submit.

2. Reflect -- Essay. Write a reflection essay about your progress in the class and especially your skill with integrative learning. Prove to yourself that you can create a great essay--appropriate for a specific audience (your instructor), rich with specific detail, and effectively crafted.
   Generating and gathering supporting materials -- Review your previous work. Have your listening, writing, and speaking skills improved? Has your attitude about speaking changed since the beginning of the semester? What parts of this class do you see as relevant to your future in college and/or career? How well did you practice integrative learning? Refer to the starred assignments and explain why you're proud of them. Refer to the integrative learning rubric. Spend some time freewriting about your accomplishments, growth, and/or realizations. Since you didn't write a self-evaluation of your final speech, address your abilities to use different strategies for listeners and readers; use your research report and persuasive speech as examples. To create your reflection essay --
   1. MAP -- Make decisions about your MAP (message, audience, purpose)
   2. Organize and format -- Observe the standard essay format: title (not the name of the assignment), introductory paragraph with a thesis, well developed body paragraphs with topic sentences, and a conclusion paragraph.
   3. Draft, revise, edit.

3. Connect Yourself, Your Goals, Your Potential Employer--Resume
   Now that you have identified your strengths and areas for improvement, consider your goals for your career. Use your audience analysis skills to consider the needs of an employer and your strategies for presenting yourself to a potential employer. Write a resume! See examples in *Writing Matters* and at the Career Center website (www.career.vt.edu). You'll use this resume as a foundation across your college career as you add items reflecting academic and professional expertise. The resume may also help you identify some gaps you need to work on next year.

Note: You may want to store your files from all of your courses in your personal workspace on Google Drive. This is good time to collect those files in case you need to refer to them during some other semester. You won't have to worry about a computer problem that results in lost files!

Appendix

Appendix A. Progress Memo

Are you progressing toward your goals in this course? At some point, you'll be asked to write a progress report. Use a progress report to reveal your accomplishments. Progress reports are useful for the reader and for the writer--you! First, the reader (your professor or boss) gets an idea of how well your project is moving along. That information may cause a shift in deadlines or resources.

Second, this process of describing your progress may serve as a little reality check about how much time you have left in the semester to accomplish certain goals. If you are working with a team, such a report can help to assure consistency among the team members.

Third, the report will also be helpful to you if you are studying with or working for someone who has a faulty memory. Just <u>telling</u> that person that your project has run into trouble may not be sufficient. If you need to change topics, spend more money, or extend a deadline, create a memo or report. Then you have some protection from the consequences of someone's faulty memory. For your future use, following is a template for a standard progress report.

Progress Report -- Template
TO: Dr. _____
FROM: Billy Joe Smythe, 11:00 class
TIME COVERED BY REPORT: (start date) through (current date)
SUBJECT: Progress Report: _____

Introduction
Provide background information about the project.
Work Completed
Use specific detail to describe some of the activities you have completed.
Present Status
Write a paragraph about your current situation.
Work Remaining
Write a paragraph about steps of the project you have yet to complete. What are your expectations? What do you want to accomplish? Have you revised your plan? Why?
Conclusion
Is the original deadline still feasible? Explain why or why not.

For this assignment, however, we'll adapt the standard format in three ways:
1. Use only brief statements for the intro and conclusion
2. Narrow the headings to three – Goals Complete, Goals in Progress, and New Goals
3. Practice using a table in a document to organize information.

Steps toward the progress memo
1. Review your goals memo from the beginning of last semester, your reflection essay at the end of the semester, your portfolio, and the syllabus for spring semester. The CommSkills II plan includes research skills, use of APA documentation, critical reading of non-fiction essays and journal articles, a complex team project, and public speaking.
2. Review any course work you have completed since August -- especially anything that might show progress toward your goals. This might include formal work that you turned in for a grade, or in-class activities in which you participated.
3. Review any independent work you've undertaken to improve those skills you mentioned in your goals memo. In the same way you might set a workout plan if you wanted to lose

weight or build muscles, you should have set an improvement plan related to your goals for this class. Have you worked through exercises in *Writing Matters*? Have you visited the Writing Center or CommLab?
4. Narrow the goals so that you can really focus on them. Avoid "improve writing" or "improve public speaking"; those are too broad. Select components of those larger competencies.
5. Create a draft with the following components:
   - standard memo heading
   - sentence about your overall evaluation of your work
   - table that reflects your goals and efforts (Use "Table" command in Word. Creating tables is an important skill that adds visual appeal to your work.)
   - 2 or 3 goals identified in each section
   - sentence or two about your predictions for success by the end of the semester
6. Revise, edit, and proofread. Submit a final draft along with any rough drafts and notes.

Memorandum Template

Note: This example is a template to be used as a model for format. Please do not copy the content of this example. Use the steps shown on the previous page to develop content unique to your situation.

To: name of instructor
From: your name
Date:
Subject: Progress in CommSkills from August 2018 to present

Opening sentence about your overall progress in the course—Pleased? Disappointed? Surprised?

Goals Completed, Fall 2018

Goals	Problem	Plan	Progress
1. Increase participation	Hesitant to contribute in class	Contribute once a week	Meeting goal most weeks (example?)
2			

Goals in Progress, Fall 2018-Spring 2019

Goals	Problem	Plan	Progress
1. Reduce comma errors	Too many commas	*Writing Matters*, exercises #___ Writing Center	Complete ex. by Feb. 1 Meet with tutor
2.			

New Goals, Spring 2019

Goals	Problem	Plan	Progress
1. Improve gestures during speeches	Become frozen in front of audience	Rehearse in CommLab before each speech	Use natural gestures to accent at least one point in each speech.
2.			

Final statement about your plan to complete your goals by the end of the spring semester. Do you need to change your approach? Are you on target?

Appendix B. Informal Feedback

Occasionally we'll use informal feedback to respond to impromptu speeches, in-class activities, or other assignments. Identify three strengths (the stars) and one wish (the question mark) about the topic or activity. We'll discuss criteria in class.

Activity _____

★

★

★

?

Name?

_____

Activity _____

★

★

★

?

Name?

Appendix C. Course Information

Acknowledgements

The course was designed and developed by Dr. Marlene M. Preston with assistance, inspiration and support from the following:

- The faculty of the Virginia Tech Department of Communication Studies endorsed and supported the original proposal and its subsequent development, demonstrating their interest in and dedication to preparing students for successful academic and professional careers.
- Dr. Rachel Holloway and Dr. Beth Waggenspack of the Virginia Tech Communication Studies Department contributed numerous ideas for the development of the course content and supported the establishment of this course.
- Faculty who have taught the course also have provided valuable feedback each semester.
- The Center for Excellence in Undergraduate Teaching funded a Summer Faculty Fellows Grant for Dr. Preston to support (1) analysis of the Spring 1997 pilot, (2) curriculum design, and (3) materials development.

Course Development

Proposal, Fall 1996

The idea for this course was first developed by Marlene Preston and the Department of Communication Studies as a proposal for a Student Success Grant during Fall Semester 1996. The grants program called for proposals that would heighten the likelihood of success for underclassmen.

The proposal--authored by Dr. Preston, edited by Dr. Rachel Holloway, and endorsed by the Department of Communication Studies--reflected concern for underclassmen as they faced the challenges of writing and speaking for college and career. The proposal focused on the development of a course that was described as follows:

> Speech Communication would focus on basic communication skills essential for student success, including group discussion, public speaking (researching, writing and delivering speeches), interpersonal communication, listening skills, and audience-centered writing. The goal of the course is to develop student skills in interacting with teams, making class presentations, and communicating with peers and professors in person and in writing. More confident communicators also develop more effective ways of working and living with peers in a university setting.
>
> As students strive to meet the revised academic eligibility requirements, they must participate more fully in their classes. Underclassmen may be particularly reluctant to share ideas, assume leadership of teams, initiate conversations with peers and instructors, or complete class presentations. Students who are accustomed to passive learning models are poorly equipped to adjust to active learning models.

The proposal led to a pilot course for Spring 1997.

One-semester Pilot, Spring 1997

As an outgrowth of that proposal, Dr. Preston designed a course that was piloted as Speech Communication (COMM 2014) during Spring 1997. A one-semester course, the class was targeted primarily to sophomores who were required to take Public Speaking. Students noted increases in their understanding of listservs, research strategies, and many modes of communication. Data collected during the course was analyzed and led to the following revision.

Two-semester Expanded and Revised Course

Because of the success of the pilot and the breadth of the material, the course was expanded. Beginning in Fall Semester 1997, freshmen enrolled in the two-semester class to meet Area 1 and Public Speaking requirements. The new course integrates writing and speaking as students study audience needs and presentation skills. Students study the process of writing and speech-building, including the use of advanced research tools. They explore their own communication styles, group interaction, and public speaking.

In Fall 1999, CommSkills moved from "special study" status to recognition within the College of Arts and Sciences as COMM 1015-1016.

In Fall 2000, CommSkills was formally accepted into Area 1 of the Core Curriculum.

In Fall 2006, CommSkills contributed to the Exemplary Department Award for the Department of Communication.

Course Design: Teaching and Learning of Discourse

Often our approach to the teaching and learning of discourse--the effective writing and speaking of our language--gets fragmented into separate Composition and Public Speaking classes. While this tradition has been evident for many years in higher education and in K-12 schooling, it has not always been so, nor does current educational literature support that approach as the only meaningful way to teach these concepts.

Based on recent research in learning theory, we know that people need to make personal connections with what they're learning. They wonder, "How does this relate to what I already know? How will it be important in my life today? How will it be useful in my studies or career in the future?" If they recognize the usefulness and connectedness of what they're learning, they're more likely to learn it. As they master new material, they make their own connections between concepts. If they see relationships between ideas, they find them easy to remember for long periods of time, certainly beyond an exam. Another key to getting those concepts into long-term memory is the actual use of the concepts -- practicing the new ideas and skills, especially in a group setting. Finally we recognize that people must learn the "rules" of a new discourse community (the writing and speaking expected in that environment) if they want to succeed.

As an outgrowth of this knowledge of learning theory, this course is designed to
- build on students' prior knowledge
- reflect the kinds of tasks students will complete in other courses
- provide challenging and relevant tasks in small steps, leading students toward mastery
- enhance students' ability to work with others as they work together to master concepts and solve problems
- ease students' transition into their new discourse communities-college and career